BOOKER AND THE BOOKER PRIZE

We are often asked at Booker why does a company whose main interests are in food, nutrition and healthcare sponsor a prize for fiction?

It is a particularly pertinent question given that the Prize in many ways is far better known to the general public both in the UK and overseas than is the company itself.

We have four answers when we are asked about our involvement with the Prize:

The first is that the Prize, like Booker businesses, is successful and is concerned with the pursuit of excellence. The Booker Prize is in the forefront of corporate sponsorship and can claim to have brought serious fiction to a wider audience. Similarly, Booker's mainstream activities such as poultry, salmon and seed breeding, mushroom growing, landscaping, cash and carry wholesaling, service to caterers, nutritional supplements and natural healthcare are leaders in their respective markets.

The second answer we give is that Booker is very proud of the success of the Prize. It is a focus of recognition to our shareholders, employees, customers and the communities we serve. It transcends the specialist audiences of our agribusiness, food distribution and health products activities and reinforces the corporate identity of a diversified group. Booker, with its interest in physical health and well-being fostered through involvement in the food chain, is committed, too, to cultural excellence, of which serious literature is a part. *Mens sana in corpore sano*.

The third answer is that the Prize accords with Booker

management style. Our businesses thrive as independent operating companies under strong specialised management within firm financial disciplines. The Prize similarly has flourished under the guidance of an independent committee representing both Booker and the book world. The company ensures value for its sponsorship but entrusts administration to those more closely connected to its beneficiaries.

The fourth answer is that Booker has enjoyed success with the development of its authors' copyrights. We have felt a corresponding obligation to promote the living word and to encourage authors.

The Prize has won the ultimate accolade of being instantly recognised throughout the world as 'The Booker'. 'The Booker' could not exist without Booker and its record of success.

Lord Campbell of Eskan, a former chairman of the company, once defined Booker 'as a group of companies worked and managed by men and women in the interests of shareholders, their fellow-employees, customers and the community'. That declaration of corporate responsibility remains the cornerstone of the Booker approach. The Booker Prize is one small fruit of the larger Booker endeavour. The Prize belongs to this Booker community as surely as it does to the distinguished contributors to this book.

Michael H. Caine

Sir Michael Caine
Chairman
Booker plc

PRIZE WRITING

PRIZE WRITING

An Original Collection of Writings by
Past Winners to Celebrate 21 years of
The Booker Prize

Hodder & Stoughton

LONDON SYDNEY AUCKLAND TORONTO

British Library Cataloguing in Publication Data

Prize writing: an original collection of writings by past
  winners to celebrate 21 years of the Booker Prize.
  I. Goff, Martyn
  823'.01'08 [FS]

  ISBN 0-340-51077-3

First published in Great Britain 1989

Published by Hodder and Stoughton,
a division of Hodder and Stoughton Ltd,
Mill Road, Dunton Green, Sevenoaks, Kent TN13 2YA
Editorial Office: 47 Bedford Square, London WC1B 3DP

Photoset by Rowland Phototypesetting Ltd,
Bury St Edmunds, Suffolk
Printed in Great Britain by
Richard Clay Ltd, Bungay, Suffolk

CONTENTS

Acknowledgements

First and foremost I am grateful to all those Booker winners who have contributed to this book, some at short notice, others pounced upon while travelling round the world. Not all have been able to write short stories or absolutely new material, but even where they have selected favourite or key passages from their own work, they have contributed an introduction or explanation of it.

Then a special thank you to Peter Straus whose idea it was; to Ion Trewin who backed it; to Roland Philipps who picked it up and ran with it when Straus had gone to other fields; and to Anna Benn.

John Murphy, a Booker director with special concern for their authors' division at the time the Prize was started; Tom Maschler, who dreamed of and campaigned for "a Booker Prize"; and Ian Norrie, formerly a member of the Management Committee and responsible for one of the most effective rule changes, have all helped me greatly with their recollections of the early days of the Prize.

Finally I would like to express my thanks to Sir Michael Caine, Chairman of Booker plc, for his encouragement and enthusiasm for this book, so closely in keeping with his attitude to the Prize itself.

INTRODUCTION

Certain objects or events, people or animals acquire the quality of a myth to which further fame – or notoriety – effortlessly attaches without a simple explanation for the transformation being available. The original Volkswagen was a sturdy, somewhat primitive car. For decades it was endowed with special qualities. The Taj Mahal is a beautiful building, but myth has anointed it with almost magical properties. So, in a lesser way, it is with prizes. For years the Prix Goncourt had the status by which all others were judged. Then, from about 1980 onwards, the Booker Prize in Britain became part achievement, part myth, with the proportions growing steadily in favour of the latter as the years went by.

What constitutes its success? For some time the amount of the Prize, starting in 1969 at £5,000 and rising, through £10,000 to £15,000, was thought to be the main ingredient. But during the last few years Whitbread, Trask and the *Sunday Express* prizes have all offered more than Booker. Then again, scandal has been cited as a strong factor. Some of these incidents will be dealt with later in this introduction, but none in news terms matches the first *Sunday Express* Prize when Auberon Waugh, one of the judges, in a speech at the reception for the winner, told how he disagreed with his fellow judges and wanted a different winner altogether!

A third reason for the Booker's extraordinary success has been sought in the careful choice and balance of judges. There has been none of Whitbread's doubtful employment of some non-reading celebrities for the last round. Every judge has been expected to read every book, unlike those prizes where entries are sieved in advance and reduced to a small quantity. Even so there have been years when the winner has seemed to many people on the literary circuit some way from being "the best novel of the year", as there have been other years that have yielded winners who are likely to be read in fifty years' time.

A fourth possibility is the structure of the management of the prize. Booker plc, a large conglomerate specialising in food, agriculture and health-care products, sponsors the Prize. But its management is carried out by a committee that consists of an author, a hardback and a paperback publisher, a bookseller, a librarian, the chairman of Booker, another senior executive from that company and the Prize's administrator. Not content with that degree of arm's length management, the actual administration of the Prize, from calling in the entries to publicising the winner, is handed over to Book Trust, an independent charitable trust whose aim is to promote reading. Is this careful system for running the Prize contributory to its success?

A fifth reason may be the change from knowing the winner a month in advance, which is what happened and was almost always leaked until 1979, and "the smoke going up on the night", as has happened ever since. The reason for reaching the decision earlier was to allow the winning publisher to reprint the book if necessary. Hampstead bookseller Ian Norrie, then on the Management Committee, urged the Committee through Michael Caine to change to the more dramatic timing. Undoubtedly this was wise advice.

I suspect that it is probably a mixture of all five reasons, added to which is that stroke of luck or timing that converts ordinary success into the making of a myth. Thereafter the myth, like a snowball running down a hillside, continues to grow automatically. If the proportions of these ingredients are difficult to establish, then the moment the resulting mixture started to transform modest success into myth is less so. For it was almost certainly in 1980, the year in which William Golding won by a hair's breadth with *Rites of Passage* from Anthony Burgess'

Earthly Powers. Whether it was the sense of two giants battling against each other or just that the seeds planted over the twelve years of the Prize's running had at last taken root, there is little doubt that the contest started to matter not just to literary circles, but to a huge number of ordinary readers, whether they were book buyers or library borrowers.

There was on that occasion a small item of supposed scandal. Anthony Burgess, who was staying at the Savoy Hotel at the time, was said to have a direct line to me at the judging. If he won, he would attend the dinner; if not, then he would stay away (mostly, I believe, because he hated the idea of having to put on evening dress). Although I did inform him by phone of the result, there was no "direct line", a feature that hardly fits into later editions of the story where he is supposed to have been waiting for my call in Monte Carlo, where he lives, before deciding whether to come. This presupposes a very fast plane indeed, since the judging ends around 6 p.m. and the dinner starts at 7.30!

But before we begin to look at some of the incidents that contribute to the ingredient that I have labelled "scandal", it might be as well to establish how the Prize started, for here too myth has ensured a number of versions. One of these has Ian Fleming, author of the Bond books published by Jonathan Cape, proposing the idea during a game of golf with the chairman of Booker. As Tom Maschler, chairman of Jonathan Cape, said: "For all I know they may have played golf together, but that is not how the idea came to Booker."

In the middle sixties Booker established a division to buy the copyright of famous authors. Ian Fleming was one of the first of these, though later the list included writers like Agatha Christie and Dennis Wheatley.

The chairman of the books division was Charles Tyrell and the managing director was John Murphy. The idea quickly proved successful both for the company and the individual authors. Tyrell and Murphy, with the blessing of the company's chairman, David Powell, began to think of ways of showing their appreciation for this success in the form of establishing bursaries, scholarships or prizes.

At this moment they were approached by Tom Maschler and Graham C. Greene, then chairman and managing director of Jonathan Cape, the distinguished literary publishing house. Maschler had long been looking for a sponsor for a major fiction prize that might one day rival the Prix Goncourt. This proposal was received enthusiastically in the light of Booker already thinking about some form of sponsorship, so the Booker Prize was born.

Initially the Publishers Association backed Tom Maschler and were not only willing to become involved as co-sponsors (money apart), but also to provide the services of Jill Mortimer from their staff to run it. The first management committee was soon set up, dominated by Maschler and Lord Hardinge of Penshurst, the latter then literary adviser to Booker apart from working as an editorial director of a publishing house. David Powell was succeeded by George Bishop as chairman of Booker, and he in his turn by Sir Michael Caine, the present chairman, in 1979. It was at that time that the somewhat *ad hoc* management committee was replaced by one representing all parts of the book world in a form that persists to this day. Sir Michael had shown a deep commitment to the Prize from 1973, even at a time when the company was under threat of takeover; and his enthusiasm has been one of the Prize's main strengths. The myth that the Booker Prize has in part become ensures that imagination records a great deal more scandal than actually happens. I am frequently told that every year something awful takes place, yet incidents have been comparatively few.

The most famous was when John Berger won the Prize with his novel, *G*. It was 1972 and there were only three judges (most years there have been five). They were Cyril Connolly (chairman), Elizabeth Bowen and George Steiner. Strongly promoted by the last-named, *G* commended itself to those who had been looking for a more experimental book to win. John Berger, however, had his own doubts. His *gracious* speech of acceptance of the £5,000 cheque explained that he had learnt that Booker sweated blacks in the West Indies. Accordingly he was unable to accept the Prize, or, rather, he would give half of it to the Black Panther movement. Leaving aside the mixed morals of keeping half a prize you feel tainted, Berger was twice out of date. While Booker no longer had sugar plantations in the West Indies, the Black Panther movement had ceased to exist two years earlier! There was another gaffe the following year. At that time Booker invited a well-known personality to hand over the cheque. On this occasion it was Lord Butler. He started his speech with two anti-semitic jokes which were particularly inappropriate as the winning publisher was a distinguished Jew.

For the following four years there were only three judges each time, while on the last of those years there was an innovation. The Management Committee had hearkened to press comment that the Prize was becoming too highbrow, too divorced from the ordinary reader. One judge ought to represent the man in the street. I was doubtful about this since one could hardly stop the first person coming along the pavement outside Booker, where the committee meets, and ask if they would like to judge a prize which involves reading some eighty or ninety books. In the event, we came up with neither a man nor someone, at the time of our asking, who matched the metaphor. The first of such judges was the Prime Minister's wife, Mary Wilson.

The chairman of the judges that year was Walter Allen, the well-known literary critic and novelist. Since paralysis unfortunately prevented him from travelling, we agreed to hold the judges' meetings at his house in Canonbury. It was also agreed that I would collect Lady Wilson from her house in Lord North Street (the Wilsons had decided not to live in 10 Downing Street during his second term as Prime Minister). I arrived there to collect her at 9 o'clock one morning. A policeman checked my identity outside the front door; another, in the hall, asked me to wait in the upstairs drawing room until Mrs Wilson was ready.

In the room I found that day's newspapers, opened at the editorial pages, spread on sofas and floor. As I was peering at one of them a huge cloud of smoke entered the room, followed moments later by the Prime Minister. He asked me who I was. I explained. He nodded and started to look at the papers. Suddenly he looked up. "How much is this prize worth that Mary is judging?" I told him. His interest was kindled. He patted

the sofa next to him. "Sit down and tell me all about it then."
His interest was maintained, too. On the night of the dinner at
Claridges, he left another dinner for the space of the sweet
course to attend the Booker presentation.

There have been other scandals, though a less emotive word
might describe them more accurately. A chairman of the judges
wrote to a well-known novelist telling him that he ought to have
been shortlisted but he had been unable to persuade his fellow
judges of the rightness of this because women were in a majority;
while, almost at the same time, his wife wrote an ecstatic letter
to one of the shortlisted authors about his book, making the
author fairly certain he would win. Malcolm Muggeridge, having
agreed to be a judge, dropped out when he read some of the
first entries: they were too sexy. And Fay Weldon, as chairman
of the 1983 judges, was required to give a casting vote in favour
of J. M. Coetzee's *Life & Times of Michael K* or Salman Rushdie's
Shame and had a miserable, wriggling twenty-five minutes doing
so. She claimed, sweetly but with low credibility, that it was
normally her husband who made the major decisions in their
lives!

There have, too, been technical difficulties. The judges
decided that V. S. Naipaul's *In a Free State* was both a novel
and the winner in 1971, but after a night's sleep John Fowles
felt uneasy about the eligibility of the book. It was a novel-length
story, enclosed in two short stories and then again enclosed in
two pieces of a journal. But his fellow judges, who included Saul
Bellow and Antonia Fraser, were not willing to change their
minds. The issue of *faction* arose again in 1982 when the winner
was Thomas Keneally's *Schindler's Ark*. Hodder and Stoughton
published it in Britain as fiction, although in the States the
Library of Congress catalogued it as non-fiction. At their shortlist
meeting the Booker judges decided that it *was* fiction. At the
final meeting they began to go back on their decision, so that I
was forced to remind them that by shortlisting it they had
confirmed its eligibility.

A more curious worry assailed the judges in 1984 over J. G.
Ballard's *Empire of the Sun*. There had been letters and articles
in the press pointing out inaccuracies in Ballard's story of the

Japanese occupation of Shanghai in the Second World War. Some judges, however, maintained that fiction was fiction so how could one talk of "inaccuracies"? In the event, and to many people's including the author's surprise, the Prize went to Anita Brookner for *Hotel du Lac*.

The judges' biggest problem, however, is not the fact or fiction one, but the definition of "the best novel of the year". It is very flexible and each set of judges will give their own interpretation. It is not, of course, the only aim of the Prize. Booker plc want to reward merit, raise the stature of the author in the eyes of the public and increase the sale of books. The rub probably comes in the third aim. Booksellers in any case regard the choice of the winner as good if the book sells well and bad if it does not. Coetzee was not a major seller in Britain so the choice of his book was not welcomed by the retail trade. To find a book that passes the tests of literary critics and academics *and* pleases the booksellers is not easy. So it is probably this that has led unconsciously to the slight seesaw effect in the annual choice: Coetzee followed by Brookner followed by Kingsley Amis; or Naipaul followed by Berger followed by J. G. Farrell. Both sides lament this when the particular winner comes from the other category, but twenty-one winners (Nadine Gordimer and Stanley Middleton were joint winners in 1974) do seem to have been shared between the two parties with some sort of rough justice.

It is clear from this that the composition of the judges is one of the Management Committee's most important tasks. Although the committee has a short post-Prize meeting to assess the year just finished, its main meeting is in February. That meeting has a standing list of possible judges to which are added any bright ideas, either of those on the committee, or from outsiders. People like Melvyn Bragg and Michael Holroyd, the latter once on the committee himself, will telephone to suggest people of exceptional merit who might have been overlooked.

The committee's first task is to find a chairman for the forthcoming year. In practice they nominate three possibilities, in order of preference, so that if I approach Number 1 and he or she says, "No, sorry, can't do it", I can then move on to

Number 2. Having put the three chairman in place on paper, the committee then tries to produce a balanced team under each of them. Inevitably the panel will be quite different if the chairman is Fay Weldon than if it is Norman St John-Stevas. Balance in each case will partly be obtained by having an academic, a critic or two, a writer or two and the man in the street; and partly by an assessment of the various personalities involved.

The committee has tried to involve overseas judges, but there are practical reasons against this. It was easy to have Professor Sam Hynes because he was spending a year in Britain. It was more difficult with Mary McCarthy, though she had only to come from Paris. It was much more difficult in the case of Saul Bellow and Brendan Gill. With five judges all from Britain, of whatever nationality, judges' meetings can fairly easily be altered when necessity demands. On top of which there is the considerable extra expense if the judge has to be flown each time from America or Australia. Booker are reasonably generous with their contribution to the Prize, but reasonably restrained at the same time.

It is above all important to be able to guarantee that all five judges will be able to attend the final meeting of the panel, the one that takes place at 4 p.m. on the afternoon of the dinner at which the Prize is presented. In 1985 Joanna Lumley was "the man in the street". She had warned me early on that she might be opening in a new play on the night of the dinner. Assuming that this was in the West End of London, I told her not to worry about it, thinking that she would be able to attend the judges' meeting from 4 to 6 p.m. and then go off to her first night. It was a shame that she would miss the dinner itself but not too terrible. What I had not realised was that the play was opening in Brighton! She missed the meeting, a book of which she was not in favour won, and the press had a high old time on the subject of absent judges.

Literary circles are full of gossip about people who have not been asked to be judges. Like all such committees, however, it only needs one member of the Management Committee to voice powerful opposition to a particular name for that name to be put on one side while the member remains on the committee. Since that committee turns over its personnel constantly but slowly the bar eventually comes off as has happened in one or two noticeable cases.

The Management Committee's other major task is to amend the rules as and when necessary. The Prize to date has been open to a citizen of the former British Commonwealth, meaning the present Commonwealth plus Eire, Pakistan and South Africa. No one has protested about the last named, though two authors known for their opposition to apartheid, Nadine Gordimer and J. M. Coetzee, have won the Prize. Indeed there has been no call to change the frontiers of eligibility from within the committee or outside it, though it is recognised that residents of long standing, like Paul Theroux and David Plante, are ineligible as American citizens.

The rule that has been the subject of much discussion and a number of changes is the one that governs the number of titles a publisher may submit. This has varied over the years and is now fixed at three, though past winners no longer count against that three. This means that Hodder and Stoughton, for example, could enter three books plus new ones by Thomas Keneally and Keri Hulme, both past winners. In addition to this, the publisher may submit a further five titles which he wants to bring to the judges' attention. These, since 1988, must be accompanied by a brief reason showing why the publisher considers them of particular merit. At the time this new version of an old rule was announced, it was also decided that the judges *must* call in between five and fifteen of the listed titles apart from those submitted. This was partly in answer to the widespread criticism in 1987 when the judges refused to call in any titles whatsoever. Finally, the judges may call in any titles that they feel should have been in the competition but which have neither been entered nor listed. Most years there are two or three entries under this rule.

While the Management Committee has bent over backwards to meet annual criticism on the question of entries, it can never be solved to the satisfaction of all parties. One only has to posit a literary publisher like Jonathan Cape to see that they will never be satisfied with a three-entry limit whereas plenty of publishers with good but limited fiction lists would be quite happy. As long as the Management Committee is resistant to the idea of having entries sieved in advance of the judges' seeing them – it is at present, and I am too! – so long will there have to be a low, restrictive number allowed.

The rest of the Management Committee's concerns are less the subject of great argument. They do care that the number of entries is still between 85 and 105 annually, making great demands on the judges' time. Both Sir Michael Caine, Booker's chairman, and I have written to publishers on a number of occasions asking them only to submit books that they believe actually have a chance of being shortlisted, but without much effect. The pressure from authors and agents is, some of them claim, too great to resist, so the books get entered.

Otherwise the Management Committee discusses the quality of the live broadcast on television. This has moved from BBC to LWT (on Channel 4) and, in 1988, back to the BBC again. Melvyn Bragg and Hermione Lee reached a high standard over their four years which BBC2 failed first time round to match, although they avoided the worst of their pre-LWT efforts when Selina Scott on camera asked one of the judges if she had by any chance read any of the books! While it is true that it is not easy to make a compelling programme in visual terms about a book prize being presented, around half a million people a year have been faithful viewers. As significant has been the way that the result of the Prize has become news in television and radio terms; and not only in Great Britain.

Finally the Management Committee discusses the dinner in all its aspects and was responsible in earlier years for the moves first from the Café Royal to Claridges, then from Claridges to the Stationers' Hall and then to the Guildhall. In the earliest years there was a reception at the Stationers' Hall rather than a dinner, but this was judged not very successful, in part because of the inadequate amplifying system for the speakers. It also approved the change to evening dress despite a few objections to this. Philip Larkin in *Required Writing* quotes from his speech as chairman of the Booker judges in 1977:

Only a few months ago Mr Martyn Goff assured me that there was no need to buy new evening clothes for this occasion, as dress was informal. It was not. In consequence I am forced to appear before you unmistakably as a writer of the fifties, a man overtaken by the Booker Award's continuing increase in status.

Now, alas, that the great poet is no longer with us, I confess that when inviting him to be the chairman I countered his "I won't do it if I have to wear a dinner jacket" by saying that he did not. Although I was technically truthful, on finding out that it was expected of him, he brought out his old, unfashionable suit.

Once the judges have been chosen and the rules finally polished the Management Committee hands the rest of the administration over to Book Trust (called the National Book League until 1986). Book Trust is responsible for the publicity and mails entry forms to publishers besides announcing the Prize in the trade press. Entries start to arrive in late April or early May, roughly at the time that I give the judges their first lunch together. While this is mainly for them to meet each other, they can also sort out administrative details and arrange the date of the shortlist meeting (or meetings). Some judges go abroad for a month or two in the summer, so arrangements have to be made for their eighty or ninety books to be posted to them in Italy or Sweden or wherever in parcels of four or five as the books arrive at Book House. Throughout the summer both the Publicity Department of Book Trust and I are at the disposal of the judges over all sorts of questions of eligibility and the like.

The closing date for entries is June 30th, but for those publishers who have sent in an entry form but who are unable to provide even proof copies for a further month and who undertake to submit finished copies as soon as they are available, that date is extended to July 31st. Around the third week in August I usually ask each judge for his or her six front runners. This in no way binds them but is used to give their fellow judges an idea of the way they are thinking. On a number of occasions a judge has re-read a book cast aside in the first instance as a result of its being another judge's choice. From those short lists something between twenty and thirty books emerge for the shortlist meetings.

Since Booker plc make all the arrangements for the dinner themselves, the remainder of Book Trust's work is to have the publicity material designed and printed, to place or suggest articles and features on the Prize in the national press and media and to publicise, in cooperation with the publishers, the shortlisted books.

I have already indicated that the Prize is now news in Australia and Canada, in America and Scandinavia, everywhere indeed where English is spoken. It is not only in the number of additional copies sold that the Booker Prize has such an effect on the winner but also in the establishment of a worldwide reputation where this did not exist before. At one leap winning the Booker with *Midnight's Children* turned Salman Rushdie into a major international literary figure. J. M. Coetzee, with a book that was considered difficult reading though mainly by those who had not tried it, had sold 5,910 copies before it was shortlisted; almost the same figure again on being listed; and a further 34,000 copies after winning. The case of Anita Brookner was even more striking. She had been selling 2,000 to 3,000 copies of her novels despite excellent reviews and publicity. *Hotel du Lac* had a first print of 4,000 which arrived in time for the book's shortlisting. By the end of the year it had sold all but 50,000 copies!

It is important to emphasise that once an author has broken the Booker barrier, then the likelihood is that his or her books, as well as all sorts of rights, will go on selling at previously undreamt of levels. Winning the Prize can be the making of an author; and even a very well-known writer like William Golding can sell a greatly increased number of copies through winning the Prize.

Clearly the Prize's first aim is being achieved. The best novel of the year in the eyes of that year's judges sells many more copies. But the Prize has other achievements. All over the country libraries and universities hold seminars and lectures that are based upon Booker winners; a West country public library even ran an alternative Booker one year. The Prize, then, not only causes great attention to be paid to the winner and shortlisted titles, but also to a number of titles that journalists and critics *thought* should have been shortlisted.

The Booker Prize in short has contributed to raising the profile of serious fiction during its twenty years of existence. It has helped to restore confidence in the form ("Is the novel dying?" has ceased to appear as a regular Sunday newspaper article); it has boosted writers in their need to find an audience; and it has acted as a signpost to the general reader indicating the more worthwhile books published every year. It does not, and indeed probably cannot, always get it right. It is hard on the non-winning, shortlisted authors. It focuses too much attention on the autumn publishing season. Even then its benefits clearly outweigh its drawbacks. It has led to a number of other prizes. It has helped to raise the status of Commonwealth fiction; and it has given great pleasure to writers and readers alike. That surely is enough for the first twenty years.

Martyn Goff
1989

P. H. NEWBY

P. H. NEWBY

P. H. Newby was born in 1918. He joined the BBC in 1949, becoming Controller of the Third Programme nine years later and remaining in that position, including its transition to Radio 3, until 1971. He stayed at the BBC as Managing Director, Radio until 1978. In that year he became Chairman of the English Stage Company, a position he held until 1984. In 1969 he won the first Booker Prize with *Something to Answer For*. In 1972 he was awarded the CBE.

No Horses

Ray Drower thought himself a bit of a tearaway but in fact he was just the usual sort of statistician who gets employed by big insurance companies. The life he might have lived, the actor he might have been, the drunken fights he might have been hauled out of! And the women! But it was all fantasy. He wore a dark suit, commuted from Guildford, was married to a doctor's daughter who thought him her social inferior (his father was a butcher) and they had one child, Penny, now seventeen or so. Having a teenage daughter disturbed Drower. Part of him wanted to open the door of the cage and let her fly out. The other part wanted the door kept shut. Eleanor, his wife, wanted to keep the girl close to her. She recognised that the world was a different place from the one she had grown up in but, nevertheless, there were limits.

It was not quite right to say that the Drowers lived in Guildford. The Drower home was in a village nearby and at weekends he liked to indulge another fantasy, that he was a countryman. He never actually walked about with a shotgun under his arm but he wore brogues and breeches, in winter had a Harris tweed overcoat and, in summer, a shirt in bright check and denim trousers. At Eleanor's modest garden parties he stood about in jeans and wellingtons as though he had been interrupted while mucking out the horses. There were, of course, no horses.

One Saturday morning Penny said a friend was coming round after lunch and both Ray and Eleanor assumed it would be one of the girls from school. But it was a youth in a black outfit and crash helmet riding a huge motorbike. Still sitting on the machine he removed his helmet and revealed a bony, straight-nosed face and very black almost silky hair from, as it might be, some gypsy forebear. Or it might be Red Indian. He was a big, strong youth as he needed to be to handle a machine that powerful. When he spoke his high, reedy voice was all the more surprising but he had an engaging grin to turn on Eleanor who was staring at him in amazement.

"This is Andy," said Penny.

Andy raised his gloved hand in salute. "I come over 'ere. What am I saying? I come *near* 'ere, Binnery way, clay-pigeon shooting. There's a chap got all the kit out Binnery way, clay-pigeon kit, you know. No time for it now since I took up motocross." He was full of himself, so confident he seemed capable of kissing Eleanor on the cheek. "This your Mum and Dad then, Pen?"

"Sorry. Yes, these are my father and mother."

"What's motocross?" Ray asked.

"You know what show jumping is you see on the box? Well, motocross is jumping without the 'orses. It's wiv motorbikes. Otherwise it's just the same. More than that, though, it's a race so you could say it was an over-the-sticks do. Jumps, obstacles, over tree trunks, along planks. Up and down 'ills. Calls for nerve and steady 'andling."

"You do it on that?" Ray nodded at the machine.

"No, you'd get yourself killed doing motocross on a bike like this. You've got to 'ave a special job with special suspension."

Andy now revealed he had a second helmet, a silver casque which was apparently intended for Penny. It became clear what the idea was; the pair were making off somewhere, Penny riding pillion.

"Definitely not," said Eleanor.

"Oh, Mummy!"

It was now Andy's turn to be amazed. "We wouldn't be away more'n an hour."

"No."

"Honest! There's no motocross today. I wouldn't go moto-cross on a Saturday. I'd just show Pen the field and the obstacles an' tha'. Then we'd go for a coffee."

"Oh, *please*, Mummy."

Eleanor was adamant. "It isn't fair, Penny. You just thought you'd bump us into it. I don't know this young man."

Penny had no motorbike outing that afternoon and perhaps she had not really expected one because she went off, relaxed and quiet and smiling, to show Andy the view from the top of the garden, content that she had at least got him into the house. Afterwards they all sat down drinking tea in the kitchen.

Andy said he was a chippy, a carpenter, who lived with his father and mother and two younger sisters on a council estate in Guildford. He worked for a contract builder and travelled about putting roof timbers in. Kid's play, he said, because a lot of the timbers were pre-cut and to measure. He was paid by the job and not by the hour; that was the way to make money. He worked fast. In the evenings and at weekends he went moonlighting to make more money. He liked good clothes. None of your rubbish and the bikes came dear. Then there was the maintenance. It was on one of those moonlighting jobs he met Penny. He was replacing rotten window frames in the home of one of Penny's friends and they'd got pally.

Ray rather liked him. There was no malice in the boy and his self-confidence was refreshing. He worked hard and had his fun. The boy could not understand why Penny was not allowed to ride pillion with him but he grinned and shrugged it off as much as to say you'll all see it my way, given time. Before he went he rode his bike round and round the yard just to show how expert he was at handling the machine.

"Look, Pen. Put it on –" he nodded at the helmet "and I'll take you round." It seemed harmless and perfectly safe. Penny, in her jeans, climbed on to the pillion, clasped him round the middle and, their two helmets swaying and turning together, they weaved their way into the orchard and through the apple trees, momentarily obscuring first one white-painted trunk and now another, so that the trees seemed to flicker in the afternoon light. To Eleanor the noise was intolerable.

"Beastly machine!" she said. "Beastly, filthy machine!"

It was not at all filthy. The machine was beautifully maintained and Ray examined it with interest. It had many times the power of the Norton he used to run when he was Andy's age. He would have liked – well, not to ride it but to sit in the saddle and fiddle with the controls.

He patted Eleanor's arm. "Penny'll be all right. It's just a phase."

It was a phase that went on and on. Andy would arrive after one of his moonlighting jobs and break in on Penny's homework. She was taking A-levels and Eleanor became more and more furious. She tried to explain to Andy what was at stake but Penny said she was on top of her work and Andy remarked he didn't hold with exams anyway.

"He's no good for you," Eleanor told Penny. "What do you find to talk about?"

"He's very lonely. He had a girlfriend and she dropped him. He's going to set up on his own."

"In motocross?"

"No, as a builder."

Eventually Andy succeeded in carrying Penny off for a whole day. He was a member of a syndicate now, the Rockets, and their motocross bikes were transported in a van. So Andy made the trip to the motocross down into Hampshire with Penny on the pillion and, in spite of promises, they were not back until after dark. They had dropped in on Andy's folk in Guildford and stayed there talking.

Normally Eleanor did not raise her voice but this time she shouted in anger. "We've been beside ourselves with worry. Andy, this is no way to behave."

"But it's only nine o'clock, Mrs Drower. Course, I'm sorry, but it's not late."

"You might at least have telephoned."

"My folk, they're not on the phone. Could 'ave gone out to a box. Yes, that's what we oughterer done. We oughterer gone out to a box, Pen."

He was in hot water but remained good humoured and grinning, plainly unrepentant and ready to keep Penny out the next weekend too if he saw fit, rather as though he assumed she would come out against her parents if necessary. It was Eleanor who thought Penny had become so wilful she might threaten to run away. Ray did not go so far – Penny was a dutiful girl – but he certainly thought Andy would push his luck and rather admired him for it. What if he'd been as uppity when he'd been Andy's age? The feeling he had missed so much in life hit Ray from time to time and never so strongly as at that moment. Why had he not cut college and gone down the Amazon in a canoe? Why had he not had passionate love affairs? Why had he not set out for Katmandu? Why had he not realised, like young Andy here, that life was there to be lived? Riding motocross and making a go at Penny weren't exactly the height of daredevilry but what had he ever done to compare?

So he was far from being as agitated as Eleanor when Penny floated the idea that she and Andy might go on holiday together. They would set off on the motorbike through France, camping as they went, and down to Marseilles where they would take a boat for Tunis. Eleanor was really churned up.

"Absolutely not," she said.

They had worked out the details. Andy produced road maps, lists of camping sites, even the times of sailing from Marseilles. Penny said her friend Milly Turner had been on a camping holiday with her parents in France and it had all been marvellous.

"That's different." Eleanor was so upset by the thought of such a holiday she was afraid she might say something really offensive to Andy, or to Penny for that matter. It was all very well forbidding the holiday but short of locking Penny up there was no real way to stop her going. What if Penny defied her and Ray?

Penny was hurt. "Don't you trust me? Is that what it's all about? You just don't understand." And so on. Nowadays young couples were always going off on holidays and nobody thought it strange.

When Ray rode his Norton all those years ago he could have taken a girlfriend on a camping holiday, he supposed. But it wasn't the done thing and the idea would not have occurred to him. Penny and this boy Andy were more adventurous than he had ever been. He asked questions about their journey. It would be crazy to travel on the *Routes Nationales*, he said. The secondary roads were more fun. Took longer but they were safer. Eleanor became more and more furious as she listened to his observations on French traffic conditions in the holiday season.

"Oh shut up, Ray. Penny's not going and that's flat."

The meeting broke up, nothing having been decided in spite of Eleanor's declaration. Later Ray was able to say to Penny, "I don't think it's on, girl. You can see how worked up your mother was."

"I'm going. I've got money in the bank." Penny had taken a grip on herself and spoke like one who had decided the jaunt with Andy had become something more than a pleasure in prospect. Now that her mother had spoken, it had become not just a pleasure but a duty.

Ray ate a sandwich one lunchtime with one of the senior actuaries, Dick Emmett, and found himself talking about Penny and her dash for freedom. Dick was an older man and had been through this sort of thing; he'd a daughter who was going off in a Land Rover with other kids from the Poly and he'd got them (and the Land Rover) round to his house to look them over. He liked what he saw and said OK to the trip – they were driving to Greece and hoping to take the ferry to Crete – but Dick's heart was not in it. In fact he was worried. Later, his daughter said that if he had vetoed the trip she would have accepted his ruling without argument.

"I thought she'd have cocked a snook. Just goes to show. It all went off all right."

"This is different. One boy on a bloody powerful motorbike. And camping."

"Could be worse. They might be hitch-hiking. Look, Ray. I've got an idea."

Dick said he was having to put off a family holiday because his father-in-law had moved into what he described as "the obviously terminal phase" at precisely the time the computer, having regard to his background (age of *his* parents at death, heavy cigarette smoker, two stone overweight, and so on) had predicted. It was a real comfort to Dick and his wife that Dad was fulfilling the orthodox actuarial parameters. So would the Drowers like to take over the villa – well, it was a sort of cabin, really – they had rented back of Golfe Juan? It would be quite a wheeze to invite this motorbike type along. The conventional wisdom was that undesirable boyfriends could be squeezed out by exposure to, as he put it, "life as lived at the manor".

Ray liked the suggestion he lived in a manor house but Dick might have been testing him so he said, "We don't live in any manor."

"You know what I mean."

The Drowers had made no holiday plans and the more Ray thought about Dick's proposal the more he liked it. When he got home he told Eleanor but she turned the idea down. "I don't think taking that young man on a family holiday would abash him in the slightest. He and Penny would be off on their own all the time and we'd be wondering what they were up to. The south of France doesn't attract me at this time of year. But the problem is solved anyway."

"What d'you mean?"

"The boy has told me he would not want to take Penny on holiday if it was against our wishes. He said he understood our position and agreed with it. Penny is livid and quite ready to cut him out of her life."

"Too true to be good," said Ray. "I mean, he's softening you up, isn't he? I mean, that boy's smart."

"He said his family were Seventh Day Adventists and that is why he never went motocrossing on a Saturday. He says they're all very religious."

"Seventh Day what?"

"It's immaterial. It's one of these sects. So when he says he wouldn't want to take Penny on a holiday without our permission my only wonder is why he'd thought it right to take an un-chaperoned girl in the first place. Assuming we'd agreed to the holiday."

Ray went off to look up the Seventh Day Adventists in an encyclopedia and came back with the view that Andy was lying, he was not a member of this American sect but had fastened on to it to sell the idea he was respectable.

"He's so ignorant he couldn't have invented this."

"If he'd said the Salvation Army I'd have swallowed it. Anyway, they're not going?"

"That's how the matter stands."

"I still think he could be stringing us along. He doesn't look like my idea of a Seventh Day Adventist."

In the weeks that followed Penny stopped being a schoolgirl and became a young woman. Ray and Eleanor were aware of some sort of change without being sufficiently sure of the transformation to talk about it. All they knew was they both felt a bit older but they were not an introspective couple and wouldn't have known how to spell it out even if they had wanted to. And the weather was so glorious. It was really hot, week after week, and the grass in the paddock went silver. Andy's visits became fewer and Penny seemed not to mind at all. She said he was on a big job in Basingstoke. There was no more aggressive talk about going away with Andy. She sat up late those stifling evenings with her A-level work and Ray was pleased but puzzled. If she and Andy had had a tiff it would have shown up in some way but Penny seemed just serene and Ray could only think that what he had said about being a Seventh Day Adventist was true and that Penny, who was not a religious girl (she had refused to be confirmed, saying she couldn't make untrue statements), had been put off. Eleanor was quite sure Penny had seen through Andy and was pleased as this was just what she had expected. No matter how much the world had changed Penny took after her mother.

She fell in with the idea of going to Golfe Juan because they had no other holiday planned and assumed, now the Andy factor had withered, Penny would make no difficulty about going too. She didn't, as it happened, and what Ray took as further evidence that Penny was no longer in the chrysalis stage, Eleanor thought over with much greater caution. That they were all, Ray, Penny and herself, going for a sweaty, crowded holiday in a rather vulgar part of France was tolerable because Penny was behaving sensibly. Dear, innocent girl just waiting for her A-level results! But was she as dear and as innocent as she seemed? Eleanor was uneasy that Penny never mentioned Andy nowadays and went about with this half-smiling, Mona Lisa expression on her face. There was something more to it than just confidence about exams. Eleanor suspected that something deeper was at work.

By taking the night ferry and driving in turns they were down to Avignon in time for dinner. They slept under mosquito nets in Villeneuve and Ray decided they would stay on and explore the country round about. When they arrived four days late at Golfe Juan Andy was waiting for them with his motorbike parked under the orange trees like a great crustacean, all tentacles, feelers, wheels and scarlet fuel tank.

The only one to show no surprise was Penny who would have been surprised if Andy had not been there. He had pitched a little tent next to the motorbike and now stood there wearing nothing but blue briefs and sandals, looking white and uncooked but hairily black on the chest.

"I was getting edgy, you know? You might've gone into the ditch." As nobody else said anything Andy went on talking and grinning. "I guess I'm as pleased to see you as that night I got Pen 'ome at nine o'clock."

"So this was the plan." Eleanor turned to Penny who said nothing but blushed when Andy went over and kissed her.

Even Ray was annoyed to think Andy and Penny had been plotting behind his back. "Did you expect him?"

"I told him where we'd be on holiday."

Eleanor would have hated to admit it but until Andy's little accident the holiday went rather well. Penny and Andy started water-skiing while Eleanor and Ray did the sights and sunbathed. Eleanor reflected this was probably the last holiday Penny would spend *en famille* and supposed she ought to be grateful the transition to independent holidays was so painless. Next year Penny would be at university and no doubt she'd be off with some college set Andy would certainly not fit into.

Andy invited them all out to supper. No argument about it, he said. They were his guests and he was picking up the bill and it was up to Ray to choose the wine. This was a reversal of what the Drowers regarded as normal behaviour but Ray said, "Fine", so they went into Antibes and ate in one of those restaurants on stilts over the water.

Andy told them the building trade back home was in a rocky state. There were lots of bankruptcies. He was all right, though. He had five thousand quid in the bank and, what's more, he knew a little builder on the way out whose goodwill he could pick up for peanuts. He had contacts.

"You know what? What makes the banks cough up isn't your books. I ain't got no books, 'ave I? It's what you are that counts. But it's not building I'd go for in the long run. It's property. Buying and selling. That's 'ow I see it. 'Ow does that strike you, Ray, and you, Eleanor? You know the works. You wouldn't be where you are if you didn't know the works."

He had started calling them Ray and Eleanor early on. Eleanor hated it but Ray did not mind. He minded the less because there were rougher diamonds than Andy who had become millionaires.

The little accident was this. Andy was water-skiing when he hit something that should not have been there and catapulted into a boat with the result he had a couple of cracked ribs and a broken collar-bone. This was catered for in the local hospital but what worried Andy was getting his motorbike back to England. He could not ride it, the state he was in.

Ray went for a walk along the front, took a coffee at a restaurant where he could sit at one of their outside tables, looked out at the blue sea and all the sailing craft and came to the conclusion that his hour had come. No doubt Andy had insurance that would take him and the motorbike back to England. But was that good enough? Life threw up challenges and this one, in his middle age, as one who had regrettably played for safety, he would not dodge. Indeed, he'd take it on with pleasure. He would ride the bike home to England himself. He was not sure he would not kill himself but the fact he was not sure meant it was a serious exploit he had in prospect; serious and pleasurable. It was not quite the canoe on the Amazon or the torrid affair with a film star but it was the most, at his age, he could reasonably expect.

Andy laughed. "You couldn't ride my bike, Ray. It's the insurance, see? The bike's only covered for me. Another bloke on it and it's all off."

He was strapped up, plaster round the top of him and his left arm in a sling. All trussed up, he said, for a cannibal roast. Like a Christmas turkey. This did not stop him going round to collect witnesses to his accident. Back home he was going to sue this water-skiing lot for damages.

Ray was able to sort out the insurance. He visited the Mairie in Cannes to make sure he had the proper travel documents. There were phone calls to Paris. It all took days and one official, in a rearguard action to delay matters further, seemed to want to take his fingerprints. When eventually the paperwork had been sorted out Ray emerged to discover Eleanor had put her foot down once again. He was not to ride the motorbike home. It could be freighted back and there would be room for all of them, Andy included, in the Volvo.

"Lot of pilfering on the railway," said Andy. "Send it freight and what 'appens? It turns up wivout the wheels!"

Ray had already taken a few turns on the bike under Andy's supervision. It was in fact easier to master than the old Norton because the kick-start worked first time and although there were five gears to play with the change was easier because of a clever foot control. There were not so many things for the hands to do as on the Norton, more for the feet, and Ray was confident he would not kill himself. Wearing Andy's riding gear and helmet he even took the bike up to Grasse and back, no longer quite rational about the ease with which he could handle the machine.

"No," said Eleanor. Penny was against him too. Andy was worried.

"You drive and I'll tail you," Ray said.

He was so determined, this was the compromise they settled on. After a couple of hours Ray felt the bike straining to get ahead and he shot past them, the poplars on both sides of the straight road shushing and shushing as he ran their gauntlet. Yes, it was unfair, even a bit cruel to leave Eleanor and the others trailing. They could not catch him because the traffic was building up. At some point he would have to stop and wait for them. The bike ran so sweetly, though, he went on and on. Wearing Andy's gear he felt impregnable and that made him ruthless. He was – well, who knows into what heroic fantasy he was led by the freedom, the sense of power, that the bike gave him?

So he roared ahead not knowing whether he would stop for the others or whether the devil had really got into him and he would keep going. Where to? He was not sure. Officially he was *en route* for Dover but there were other possibilities. Marseilles? The boat to Tunis? He just wanted to make up for the fun he had missed and wanting it more the farther ahead he rode.

BERNICE RUBENS

BERNICE RUBENS

Bernice Rubens was born in 1928. In 1947 she married Rudi Nassauer, who is also a novelist. They have two daughters. In 1970 she won the Booker Prize with *The Elected Member*. Apart from being a prolific novelist, she has also directed documentary films and won the American Blue Ribbon Award for the film *Stress*. She plays the piano and cello.

The Collector Who Collected Himself

There's nothing wrong with hobbies. They're things that on the whole, one grows out of. But not Vincent Gibbons. By no means did Vincent grow out of his little hobby. Rather he grew into it. Indeed, it took him over. Completely. What was once a hobby became an obsession.

It all started in his childhood. Vincent's pastime was not that of an ordinary seven-year-old. He didn't collect stamps or train numbers, model cars or aeroplanes. Nothing healthy and boring like that. Young Vincent was a widow-collector. No less. It's possible that he didn't like women very much and felt that widows were back on a shelf they should never have left in the first place. Psychiatrists, who know everything about everything, would have attributed Vincent's obsession to the fact that, in his infancy, his own mother had left him, and that it was Vincent's lifelong need to punish all women thereafter. Not that he wanted to kill them off. In which case he would have collected widowers instead. But that he wanted to witness their survival, their helplessness, their rejection. There was no relish in punishment unless it could be constantly viewed. Killing lacked grace and cunning. It was too swift and forebore contemplation. No, it was the constant spectacle of women's misery that kept Vincent very happy.

As a child, Vincent's pickings were naturally thin on the ground. In High School he had the luck to fall in with the French mistress, recently widowed and still in her weeds. It was not so much luck as cunning manoeuvre. A collector must have a modicum of the former, certainly, but it is the latter that will finally determine the quality and value of his collection.

Vincent had to choose between studying French or German.

The German mistress was happily married and that was enough to put Vincent off the language completely. But alas, the French class was already over-subscribed. So he approached Madame Chauvel in personal appeal. He knocked and entered her room and like a cautious lepidopterist, he cast his net. Now Vincent was a good-looking lad with an irresistible charm which, even in those days, was consciously sexual. Of this he gave Madame Chauvel a gentle and compelling overdose. He first expressed his sorrow at her recent bereavement. She responded gratefully, moved by his young concern. He noted how her long fingers fluttered, as if expectant of the two pins that would finally nail her in his butterfly drawer. And gladly she welcomed him as a pupil. Madame Chauvel was Vincent's first serious find. But not just an ordinary specimen. Young as she was, and beautiful and rare, he labelled her his Painted Lady, caught out of season. Not bad for starters. Thereafter, as a pupil, Vincent gave Madame Chauvel a pretty rough time. Once having nailed her to his mast, he shut the drawer on her for weeks. For weeks he ignored her presence and then, in recollection of her beauty, he would stare at her for hours in mute and humble adoration. Poor Madame Chauvel didn't know which treatment she preferred, for both were a torment to her. Moreover, both were unpunishable. For young Vincent was very clever. His behaviour stopped just short of insolence. In no way could he be deemed accusable.

As he grew older, his collection degenerated into run-of-the-mill. Brimstone stuff, Common Blue, Tortoiseshell. He cast his net in bars, dance halls and on beach promenades. The end of season at Brighton was always a happy hunting ground. But as he grew older he noticed that he had to go a-hunting less and less. His quarry often came to him and more or less pleaded capture. But Vincent had grown fussy. He wouldn't settle for any old widow. He had collected plenty of those in his time. Now he would bestir himself only for that which was special. And that which was special, was rare. Rarity ruled out heart-attack widows; such were two a penny in Vincent's ageing circle. Likewise the "merry" widows, who were unnervingly legion. Rare, and closest to special was the young, almost virgin widow, on whom Vincent had fortunately been baptised. But rarest of all was the suicide widow, the Purple Emperor, as it were, and Vincent was drawn to her like a moth to a flame. For such a specimen gave off an air of illegality, as if she were a gate crasher on the widow scene. There was something about her not quite respectable, not licitly qualified, as if she had bought her widow-of-arts degree under the counter. It was at his sixtieth birthday party, wall to wall widowed in every hue, that Vincent spotted the great prize.

Penny Black was her name and her station. A collector's item. She was a suicide widow of recent standing. Though she sat most of the time, her melancholy knees peeped below the hem-line of her black skirt. Penny Black had been coming to Vincent's birthday parties for many years. But usually as a grass widow. Her husband Paul, more often than not, was out of the country on some political assignment for his newspaper. Paul had been Vincent's closest friend, and his death had affected him deeply, a factor which seasoned his Penny obsession. When Paul had returned from his last assignment – a war report that had left him deeply depressed – things had gone radically wrong. And this year, Penny was a widow for real. He went over to the couch where she was sitting, and took her hands. She gazed at him mournfully and he was pleased.

"Can I take you to dinner one evening?" he said. "Time you got out a bit more."

She seemed pleased with the suggestion and readily agreed. She wanted to talk to him about Paul, she said. She needed to. It would calm her a little. It might perhaps help close the wound.

"Gladly," Vincent said. Words could close wounds, he thought, and those same words could open them too. A slow process, given the space between those words; the odd piece of information thrown in here and there, information to which only he, as Paul's friend, was privy. Thrown in for her solace yet, with careful presentation, guaranteed to aggravate her pain. Oh there was an art in it, that verbal torture, an art in which Vincent had had much practice. He looked forward to their first meeting.

He took her to his club. It was ladies' night and a particularly coupled event. He wanted to remind her of what she was missing. She remarked on it sadly as soon as she entered the dining-room, and he offered her an apology, full of meek humility, and readily suggested that they go elsewhere, for the hurt had already been affected.

"It's not your fault," she said as she would often say over the next few weeks when he had engineered a particular form of torment, and Vincent was pleased with his cunning.

Now Penny Black was not a stupid woman, but she was entirely hoodwinked by Vincent's seeming concern. Each night, after leaving him, she wondered why she felt so despondent, but it did not occur to her to ascribe her depression to Vincent's constant solicitude. Weeks of wooing followed, and in his own time, having reduced her into total dependence on his therapy of solace, Vincent asked for her hand in marriage. It was three months after his sixtieth birthday and half a year into Penny's widowhood. He reckoned the intervals were decent enough. And so did Penny. They married quietly and he went to live with her in his old friend's home. Once the honeymoon was over, a week in Paris, during which time he let her off his caring hook, they returned home and Vincent planned his campaign. Its essence was gentleness, the sword in the silk glove.

One night he asked her how Paul had died. Over a week of nights he ornamented that question, as she, in her turn, ornamented her replies, until he felt that the time was ripe to visit the site of Paul's departure. By that time, the tale of Paul's topping had become almost mythical and, in view of that, Penny thought that she was strong enough to share that dreaded site with Vincent. Though Vincent knew the effects of it would be mind-curdling, he took her hand with relish. They climbed into the loft.

There was nothing very imaginative about Paul's method of quietus. It was simply the old banal rope trick, hooked to the attic beam with a chair set underneath that was kicked away in a moment of desperate indecision. The rope still hung there, and the chair was there too, lying on its side, exactly as Paul had left it. She gave a little scream, and Vincent took her hand, his heart soaring. He gave her a break after that, but hinted that they do it again. It would bring all three of them closer together.

Vincent laid low for a while, and before he entered the second stage of his campaign, he took Penny on holiday to give her the strength to face her next ordeal. When they returned from Deauville, he urged her to open the door of Paul's study, a door that had been kept firmly shut since his death.

"It's part of your rehabilitation," he said.

So together each night, they went hand in hand into Paul's room. He would sit her at the desk, his arms around her shoulders, in a caress to offset her shivering. He would urge her to read Paul's work aloud, including the byline of his name. This last was a winner, for she dissolved in tears on each pronouncement.

"We must begin to use this room," Vincent said gently, for he needed access to Paul's desk for what he had in mind. So whenever Penny went out, he would ensconce himself in Paul's study and sit at his typewriter. From a perusal of his copy, Vincent gathered that Paul was an inaccurate typist, but clearly a fast one, for his errors were due to impatient speed. Often the words ran into each other, the space bar having been struck too gently to register the gap between. Sometimes he'd typed "½" instead of a full stop, since those two keys were adjacent. And often he'd typed a "9" instead of a bracket, having failed to press the capital key. With these idiosyncrasies in mind, Vincent typed his missives on Paul's yellow paper.

"It was all your fault. I hope you8re satisfied," was the first one. Simple, straightforward, and possibly, Vincent thought, true. "I hope you learn to live withit," was the second message. The third was rather more ambitious. "My love for you was too much to bear." He rather liked that one, and was inspired to type many more, each one more gruesome than the last. Then he rubbed the little messages with some dust from off the desk in order to age them a little, folded them and put them in his pocket. Their placing needed strategy and timing. He put the first in her handbag drawer. That night they would go to dinner at his club, and on such occasions she invariably used an evening bag. He opened the drawer and placed her evening bags beneath her everyday ones, laying the message casually between.

In the evening Penny went to her room to dress, while Vincent paced the drawing-room waiting for the shit to hit the fan. It came in a low and terrible moan. He rushed upstairs panting with cunning concern. The effect was more than he had dared wish for. She actually fainted with guilt and his solicitude knew no bounds. She was too disconsolate to go out that evening, and he sat with her and relished her depression. Occasionally he comforted her with kisses. She liked that. Her appetite in those quarters surprised him. And disgusted him too. He had little sexual hunger for Penny or indeed for any other woman. His total ineptness in such matters he excused with his contempt. There was nothing wrong with him, he assured himself. It was women who made the whole business so repulsive. But he could, without difficulty, cover her with kisses while shutting his eyes and thinking of butterflies. Over the next few weeks, and with considered discrimination, he planted Paul's yellow farewells about the house. Sometimes he himself would come across one in Penny's presence and he would quickly hide it, but not until she had caught him at it.

"What are you hiding?" she would ask.

"It's nothing," he said.

"It's one of Paul's, isn't it?"

"Yes," he said quickly, "but ignore it. It will only upset you."

"I want to see it."

He tried, but not very hard, to keep it away from her. Then he would view her tears with deep satisfaction and with words of comfort, groaning with concern.

A few weeks later, Vincent had to make a journey to Scotland to view and appraise a collection of antiques, for such was his line of business. He vaguely knew the owner from former transactions. Since last meeting her, she had become a widow, but an ordinary heart-attack one and of no specific interest. But he could practise on her as a pianist would on a dumb piano. He would be away for a week and hopefully he would return with an armoury of agony and anguish.

After a few days of her grass widowhood, Penny began to wonder about her sense of well-being. The backaches and headaches that had plagued her since their marriage, now suddenly ceased, and she was perilously near to making the connection, for it seemed to her that Vincent's heedfulness and her own melancholy seemed to go hand in hand. Her thoughts aggravated her already well-entrenched feelings of guilt that had been so carefully nourished by Vincent's solicitude and she decided that she wronged him and must now make up for her ungenerous surmise. She would sort out his clothes, she decided, and take them to the dry-cleaner's so that they would be pristine on his return.

In the trouser-pocket of his flannels, she found strips of yellow paper. Her heart fluttered at the sight of Paul's colour. And then she read the sundry messages within the folded strips, variations of those hateful arrows she had found, and even Vincent had found, from time to time, amongst her clothes and books. She fought against her thoughts. She dared not face the truth of it. But there was no doubt in her mind that the cunning author of those yellow barbs was at this moment besporting himself in Scotland.

She had to sit down. She tried not to think, but despite herself, all the events of her short marriage crowded into her mind, and in the light of what she had discovered, they now found their own and terrible logic. The visits to the attic, the acclimatisation of Paul's study, the terrible yellow messages, all were part of a grand plan of punishment. She was married to a maniac, and she shivered. Her first thought was to throw out all his belongings, and to change the locks on the door. But she was too angry to let him off so lightly. She was too angry too, to plan an act of revenge. For that was what she wanted. But such a plan needed to be formulated in the cold light of morning, and not now as the dusk was drawing in with its magnifying shadows. She hardly slept that night, but as soon as the light filtered through her bedroom window, she showered and refreshed herself and went for a long walk. By the time she returned she had made up her mind. There was but small preparation for her plan, and this she carried out on the eve of his homecoming.

He was due early in the morning, a factor that favoured her arrangements, for it would be light and with no need of electricity. Before going to bed that night, she turned off the main fuse, and by the light of a torch and the help of a spanner, she tore the electric blanket out of the skirting-board. The socket was already loose and in any case needed repair. Its great advantage for her purpose was that it didn't have its own switch. It simply operated on the switch attached to whatever appliance it catered for. When she'd finished, the three naked wires stuck out from the skirting board like offended question marks, and although the main switch in the fuse box was turned to "Off", she kept well clear of them. In the morning she checked the lights, but none glimmered. All was ready.

Vincent arrived early, having taken the overnight sleeper, and she had breakfast prepared. He asked for toast, as she had expected, and she had to explain the state of their electricity. She had used the blanket plug for the Hoover, she said, and had pulled it out rather sharply, so that the whole contraption had come off the wall. She had turned the electricity off at the mains in order to be on the safe side. He praised her caution and said that he would mend it right away. He could do with some toast for breakfast.

He got out his tool box, or rather, Paul's. Paul had been a great do-it-yourself man, and Penny smiled. There was some rough poetic justice about it all. She was relieved that she entertained no second thoughts. He opened the kitchen cupboard to check that the main switch was off. He double-checked too on the lights.

"Must be careful," he said, as he made his way into the bedroom. "That connection is power."

She did not go with him. She just watched the back of him and whispered farewell. She noticed that the turn-ups of his old-fashioned trousers were slightly frayed. For a moment the sight of such frailty threatened her resolve, but she steeled herself and took up her position by the kitchen cupboard. At the ready.

"How is it dear?" she shouted after a while.

"All right," he said. "I'm just about to connect the wires."

She reached up and fondled the fuse box with her fingers. Then in pre-curdled blood, she threw the switch. She went quickly to the sink and ran the tap at full force. She did not want to hear the lightning. But it streaked into the kitchen and stuttered a coiled scream. She turned off the tap and heard its whimpering coda. Then a deep groan. Afterwards, silence. She listened to that for a while, then dared to call his name.

"Is everything all right, Vincent?" she shouted, knowing that everything was all very wrong. She was unsurprised by the continued silence. Then, in her caution, she went to the cupboard and switched off the mains. She called his name again before she finally dared the bedroom. On her way the phone rang and startled her. Everything must appear to be normal, she thought, so she answered it without hesitation. It was for Vincent. She explained that he was busy mending a fuse and could he call him back? That was settled, and she was pleased because it offered her some sort of cover should cover prove necessary. "What a tragedy," she heard their friends say. "And such a happy marriage."

"Vincent?" she called yet again, and then went straight into the bedroom.

He lay on the floor alongside the bed, one fist clenched over the wires. The other hand was enmeshed in the crocheted counterpane that he had clearly clutched at in his final agony. Now it lay over him like a white net trapping an ageing and very mundane butterfly. She did not touch him, nor did she take a second, closer look. She simply shut the door behind her and phoned for the doctor.

Penny gave a party on the day that Vincent would have been sixty-one. All the regulars were there, though slightly diminished in number, and the status of widowhood was more predominant than ever before. What a pity Vincent isn't here, they said. And pity it was indeed, for he would have adored Penny and lovingly would he have cast his net. For she was a veritable Lizzie Borden, a Blackhair Streak, a Bath White even, and no widow collector could have done better than that. Though in a way, Vincent *had* collected her. He himself had birthed her though, like the salmon, he had forfeited his life in his spawning.

J. G. FARRELL

J. G. FARRELL

J. G. Farrell was born in Liverpool in 1935 and spent a good deal of his life abroad, including periods in France and Ireland, and some time in the Far East to research the background of his earlier novels. He went to live in County Cork in April 1979 where only four months later he was tragically drowned in a fishing accident.

Troubles, first published in 1970, won the Geoffrey Faber Memorial Prize, and *The Siege of Krishnapur* was awarded the Booker Prize in 1973. *The Singapore Grip*, published in 1978, completes the trilogy. His final novel, *The Hill Station*, was published posthumously in 1981, and incorporates the diaries he kept during his research for *The Siege of Krishnapur*.

John Spurling writes:

Jim Farrell died at the age of forty-four in 1979. *The Siege of Krishnapur*, which won him the Booker Prize in 1973, was his fifth novel. The first three, published at two year intervals in the sixties, had contemporary settings. It was in *Troubles* (1970), set in a huge, decaying hotel in Ireland in the twenties, that he discovered the fictional advantages of history. The overall view was higher and clearer; the details of human behaviour looked still more fantastical when they belonged to another age and society; yet the essential motive forces – greed, selfishness, altruism, fear, courage, love, idealism, etc – were identical to our own. All three of his completed historical novels – *Troubles*, *The Siege of Krishnapur*, and *The Singapore Grip* – focused on particularly ticklish episodes in British Imperial history, when the British people's sense of their own superiority to all other races and societies – and indeed the English upper middle-classes' sense of *their* superiority even to their own superior countrymen – were tested to destruction, in rebellious Ireland, mutinous India and Japanese-invaded Singapore. All three places, incidentally, had family connections for Farrell: his Anglo-Irish parents had married in India and returned to live in Ireland after the Second World War; and his father, before he married, had worked in Singapore.

The Siege of Krishnapur is based, of course, on the 1857 Siege of Lucknow, but it contains many other elements and its theme is less the heroism of the defenders – though that is certainly not denied or even, ultimately, mocked – than the inadequacy and folly of certain accepted notions. Some of these – such as Dr Dunstable's ideas of the proper way to treat cholera or the Padre's pre-evolutionary ideas about God's part in the Creation

– are now antiquated, but others, such as the Collector's belief
in scientific progress or George Fleury's romantic belief in the
primacy of "feelings", still have their adherents. As for the
central ideology – British superiority – that was not yet dead in
1973, though wilting somewhat, and may not even be entirely
dead yet.

Mr Hopkins, the Collector (in charge of the district surrounding Krishnapur), and young George Fleury (a would-be poet
who happens to be visiting India at the time of the Mutiny) are
the central characters of the novel, both sympathetic dreamers
with the capacity to act sensibly and effectively when the need
arises. The other main character in this chapter, which is the
climax of the book, is Fleury's friend Harry Dunstable, an
artillery officer, whose sister, Louise, eventually marries Fleury. Ram is an Indian pensioner loyal to the British and Ford is
a European railway engineer. The area of Krishnapur being
defended against the mutinous sepoys of the Indian Army consists now only of two main buildings, the Residency and the
banqueting hall, since the Cutcherry (court-house and administrative offices) had to be abandoned and blown up during an
earlier assault.

"The possessions" stuck in the mud rampart – and indeed
many of the outlandish weapons which occur in this chapter –
have formed a *leitmotif* throughout the book: they are the rem-
nants either of the great clutter of furniture and other objects
brought with them by the fugitive Europeans or of the particular
collection of strange inventions and idealistic works of art assembled by Mr Hopkins (Collector in two senses) after the
Great Exhibition in London in 1851. For him this exhibition and
its contents represented the onward march of science and
civilisation, for the other Europeans their possessions simply
proclaimed their own status and material well-being. But when
the monsoon rains began to wash away their earth ramparts, all
these precious things had to be sacrificed to hold the mud
together and now, in the last resort, even the Collector's
prized sculpture, *The Spirit of Science Conquers Ignorance and
Prejudice*, must be turned into grape-shot.

The chapter is, I think, the most sustained and concentrated example in Farrell's work of his unique recipe of horror, fantasy, farce and narrative energy. There is only space here to print about half of it (I have indicated the cuts with dots inside square brackets), but what the chapter does not contain, even in its full version, is the longer view, the sense of sadness and seriousness which hangs over the story as it is told from our distance in time, so it's perhaps worth quoting one of the narrator's reflections from an earlier chapter:

". . . even if a relief now came, in many different ways it would be too late . . . and not only because so many of the garrison were already dead; India itself was now a different place; the fiction of happy natives being led forward along the road to civilisation could no longer be sustained."

After this chapter, though, the relief does come and the General of the relieving army, who has naturally learnt nothing from the experience since he hasn't been involved in it, is shocked by what he finds: "He had never seen Englishmen get themselves into such a state before; they looked more like untouchables."

Extract from *The Siege of Krishnapur*

Just before dawn the sound of a voice singing came over the
darkened expanse of what had once been the Residency compound from the direction of what had once been the Cutcherry.
It was a beautiful sound. It had a strange and thrilling resonance,
as if the singer were standing in a large room or a courtyard
built of stone in one of the ancient palaces left by the Mogul
emperors further to the west. But, of course, there was no
place, nor even a large room, unless the Cutcherry cellar had
somehow survived. It could only be some quality in the stillness
of the air which made the voice carry so beautifully. Fleury
asked Ram what the song was.

"It is the name of God, Sahib," said Ram respectfully. As the
old pensioner listened to the song, which was now accompanied
by the ringing of bells, Fleury saw an expression of tender
devotion come over his lined face, and he, [. . .] thought
[. . .] what a lot of Indian life was unavailable to the English-
man who came equipped with his own religion and habits. But
of course, this was no time to start worrying about that sort of
thing.

Instead, Fleury looked to his armament, which was impress-
ive; it included a sabre, unbearably sharp, a couple of wavy-
bladed daggers from Malaya, and another, Indian, dagger
[. . .] with two blades and a handle for the whole fist,
like that of a hand-saw. Lastly he had picked an immense,
fifteen-barrelled pistol out of the pile rejected by the Collector.
This pistol was so heavy that he could not, of course, stick it in
his belt; it was all he could do to lift it with both hands. But he
had been so enthusiastic about it that he had willingly gone
through the laborious loading of its honeycomb of barrels, one
after another, and now it was ready to wreak destruction. He
already saw fifteen sepoys stretched in the ground and himself
standing over them with this weapon smoking in his hand . . .
or rather, in both hands.

[. . .]

In spite of his physical weakness Harry was busy. The balus-
trade beside him looked like the shelves of a hosiery shop:

dozens of pairs of silk stockings hung from it or lay in piles on the flagstones beside the brass six-pounder. If you had lifted the dresses of the Krishnapur ladies on that morning of the last assault, you would have found them correspondingly bare-legged, for it was they who had donated their stockings to help solve Harry's difficulty with his brass cannon . . . Because, incredible though it may seem, he had fired so many round shot in the course of the siege that the muzzle had been hammered into an ellipse. Such was the distortion that the muzzle would no longer accept round shot; nor would it have accepted canister had not Harry had the idea of tapping the canisters and using silk stockings to contain the iron balls. Beside the brass six-pounder there stood another six-pounder, this one of the iron with a longer chase. This cannon, too, had been fired a great deal and although its muzzle had shown no distortion Harry had an uneasy feeling that it might soon be about to burst.

The Collector had gone up to join Ford on the roof because he wanted to be in a position from which he could give the order to retreat at the right moment; in his own mind there was no doubt but that he would have to give it sooner or later. But the cannons on the north-facing ramparts had an essential function if the garrison was to survive the morning; these cannons must break the impetus of the first enemy attack. It was now just light enough on the roof for him to see to load his pistols. He sat cross-legged in the native fashion beside the parapet and listened to the flag stirring restlessly in the light airs above him. [. . .]

The Collector had expected that the attack would begin with the howling war cry he had come to dread, but for once it did not; out of the thin ground mist that lingered in a slight dip in between the churchyard wall and the ruins of the Cutcherry, the shapes of men began to appear. Then he heard, faintly but distinctly, the jingle of a bridle. He stood up shakily, then shouted: "Stand to! Prepare to fire!" From the roof his voice echoed over the sleeping plain like that of the muezzin. When they heart it the sepoys threw back their heads and uttered a howl so piercing, so harrowing that every window in the Residency must have dissolved if they had not been already broken.

With that, bayonets glistening, they began to charge, converging from every angle of the hemisphere; before they had advanced a dozen yards squadrons of lancers had overtaken them racing for the ramparts.

The Collector waited until he estimated their distance at two hundred yards and shouted: "Fire!" This was at the limit of the effective range of canister but he could afford to wait no longer; his men were so weak, their movements so sluggish that they would need every extra second if they were to re-load and fire another charge before the enemy reached the ramparts. As half a dozen cannons flashed simultaneously at the ramparts, gaps appeared in the ranks of charging men and horses thrashed to the ground . . . But the Collector could see that he had given the order to fire too soon. Not enough damage had been done . . . It was like watching leaves floating on a swiftly flowing river; every now and then one of the leaves would be arrested against a submerged rock while the great mass of them flowed by even faster on each side. And he could see that the distance was in any case too short: his cannons would never be able to re-load in time. He ought to have waited to fire one really effective salvo at close range. The enemy *sowars* were already on top of the ramparts.

"Spike the guns!" he shouted, but no one could possibly have heard him. Half the men were already straggling back into the Residency building or into the hospital in order to form a new position while the remainder did their best to hold off the sepoys who were already swarming over the ramparts. Some of the sepoys were shot or cut down as they struggled to get over "the possessions" which stuck out jaggedly here and there; a *sowar* pitched headless from his horse on to a silted-up velvet chaise longue; a warrior from Oudh dived head first in a glittering shower through a case of tropical birds while a comrade at his elbow died spreadeagled on the mud-frozen wheels of the gorse bruiser. But this did not delay the charge for more than an instant. More sepoys poured forward over the bodies of their fellows and a number of the defenders who had lingered too long hammering nails into the vents of the cannons were cut down as they tried to make their way back to the shelter of the buildings; many more would have perished had not a small rescuing party which included Rayne, Fleury, half a dozen Sikhs and a couple of Eurasian clerks, wielding sabres and bayonets, surged forward in a sudden counter-attack to surround their companions and drag them back. Fleury, of course, had no business being there at all, but Harry had sent him to the Residency with a message and while passing by he had found the defence so desperately hard pressed that he had forgotten all about Harry. [. . .]

"Get under cover!" yelled the Collector from the roof, not that anyone could possibly hear him. He and Ford had a cannon on the roof loaded with everything that they had been able to lay their hands on: stones, penknives, pieces of lightning-conductor, chains, nails, the embossed silver cutlery from the dining-room, and even some ivory false teeth, picked up by Ford who had seen them gleaming in the undergrowth; but the greater part of the improvised canister was filled with fragments of marble chipped from *The Spirit of Science Conquers Ignorance and Prejudice*. Naturally they were anxious to fire this destructive load before it was too late; the angle of the chase was depressed to such an extent that they were afraid that in spite of the wadding the contents of their canister might dribble out . . . already a fountain of glass marbles commandeered from the children had cascaded about the ears of the defenders.

By this time the last of the garrison had fought their way back into the buildings and were trying to defend doors and windows against a swarm of sepoys. The Collector nodded to Ford who was standing by with the portfire. Ford touched it to the vent. There was a flash and a deep roar, followed by utter silence . . . a silence so profound that the Collector was convinced that he could hear two parakeets quarrelling in a tamarind fifty yards away. He peered over the parapet. Below nothing was moving, but there appeared to be a carpet of dead bodies. But then he realized that many of these bodies were indeed moving, but not very much. A sepoy here was trying to remove a silver fork from one of his lungs, another had received a piece of lightning-conductor in his kidneys. A sepoy with a green turban had had his spine shattered by *The Spirit of Science*; others had been struck down by teaspoons, by fish-knives, by marbles; an unfortunate *subadar* had been plucked from this world by the silver sugar-tongs embedded in his brain. A heart-breaking wail now rose from those who had not been killed outright.

"How terrible!" said the Collector to Ford. "I mean, I had no idea that anything like that would happen."

But Ford's reply was to clutch his ribs and stagger towards the parapet. He had toppled over before the Collector had time to catch his heels.

But already a fresh wave of sepoys was pouring over the ramparts and bounding forward to the attack over that rubbery carpet of bodies. The Collector knew it was time he hurried downstairs . . . he had expected that something like this would happen, but not so quickly. He had not reckoned with the fact that the second charge of canister could not be fired. Just as he was leaving the roof there was a crack which stung his eardrums and the flagpole, struck near the base by a round shot, came down on top of him dealing him a painful blow on the shoulder. He found himself struggling on his back with the stifling presence of the flag wrapped round him like a shroud [. . .].

Downstairs, the Sikhs, the Magistrate, Rayne, a couple of young ensigns, and a motley collection of indigo planters and Eurasians, were engaged in a desperate fight to keep the sepoys out of the building; but already they were being driven back from doors and windows. The Collector had fortunately laid a plan to meet this contingency. He had ordered the men at the north-facing ramparts and the churchyard wall to fight their way back through the Residency from room to room towards the hall, from where a dash could be made for the head of the connecting trench; once safely inside the trench the north-facing cannons of the banqueting hall, firing over their heads, could give them covering fire to complete their withdrawal. [. . .]

Fleury, unaware of the Collector's plans for a graduated retreat because he was not supposed to be in the Residency anyway, had dashed upstairs carrying the fifteen-barrelled pistol with which he was hoping to do battle from the upper storeys. [. . .] He hurried down the corridor to the music-room. That should do fine. [. . .] He hefted the pistol toward the window, laid it on the sill, cocked it, put a percussion cap beneath the hammer, directed it at some sepoys trotting below, and pulled the trigger, confident that a sepoy would throw up his arms and sink to the ground. There was a crack, but no sepoy dropped dead; the percussion cap had fired but not the pistol. Fleury uttered a curse and started to examine it, for the life of him he could not see what was the matter. Soon he was absorbed in the workings of the pistol, which was designed according to principles that were new to him. He would not be surprised to find that by using his intelligence he could add one or two significant improvements to this design. [. . .]

Downstairs, the Collector was becoming desperate. He had just heard the banqueting hall cannons fire, which must mean that the sepoys were attempting an attack from the flank; he hoped that their attack had not succeeded because he and his men had more than they could cope with already. It was not that his plan of fighting from room to room was not working . . . on the contrary, it was working to perfection: every room they retired from was crammed with dead and dying sepoys. The only trouble was this: the sepoys kept on bravely coming forward, while he and his men kept on retreating. [. . .]

Upstairs, Fleury had taken the pistol to pieces (as far as it could be taken to pieces which did not seem to be very far) and put it together again. He did not believe himself to be any the wiser as regards the reason for it not firing, but he thought he might as well try again.

"I say, you don't happen to know how this blessed thing works, do you?" he asked the person who had just come into the music-room. But he did not wait for a reply before throwing himself to one side as a sabre whistled down and buried itself deep in the brickwork of the window sill where he had been sitting. Somehow a burly sepoy had found his way into the music-room; this man's only ambition appeared to be to cut Fleury in pieces. Luckily, the blade of the sabre had snapped off and remained embedded in the wall, giving Fleury time to aim the pistol and pull the trigger. But this time there was only a disappointing click; not even the percussion cap fired. Never mind, Fleury had plenty of other weapons. He was now trying to drag one of the wavy-bladed Malayan daggers out of his belt, which was actually a cummerbund; he was having difficulty, though, because the corrugated edges had got caught in his shirt. Well, forget about his dagger, where was his sabre? His sabre, unfortunately, was on the other side of the sepoy (it was a good thing he had not noticed it because it was so sharp that he would have been able to slice Fleury in two without even pressing). Fleury had no time to draw his final weapon, the two-bladed Indian dagger, for his adversary, it turned out, was no less impressively armed than he was himself and he was already flourishing a spare sabre which he had been carrying for just such an emergency.

In desperation Fleury leapt for the chandelier, with the intention of swinging on it and kicking the sepoy in the face. But the chandelier declined to bear his weight and instead of swinging, he merely sat down heavily on the floor in a hall of diamonds and plaster. But as the sepoy lunged forward to put an end to the struggle he stumbled, blinded by the dust and plaster from the ceiling, and fetched up choking on the floor beside Fleury. Fleury again rolled away, tugging at first one dagger, then the other. But both of them refused to yield. His opponent was clumsily getting to his feet as Fleury snatched a violin from a rack of worm-eaten instruments (the survivors of an attempt by the Collector to start a symphony orchestra in the cantonment), snapped it over his knee and leapt on to the sepoy's back, at the same time whipping the violin strings tightly round the sepoy's neck and dragging on them like reins.

The sepoy was a large and powerful man, Fleury had been weakened by the siege, the sepoy had led a hard life of physical combat, Fleury had led the life of a poet, cultivating his sensibilities rather than his muscles and grappling only with sonnets and suchlike . . . But Fleury knew that his life depended on not being shaken off and so he clung on with all his might, his legs gripping the sepoy's waist as tight as a corset, his hands dragging on the two broken pieces of violin. The sepoy staggered off, clutching at the violin strings, out of the music-room and down the corridor with Fleury still on his back. He tried to batter his rider against the wall, scrape him off against a fragment of the banisters, but still Fleury held on. They galloped up and down the corridor, blundering into walls and against doors, but still Fleury held on. The man's face had turned black, his eyes were bulging, and at last he crashed to the ground, with such force that he almost shook Fleury off . . . but Fleury remained dragging on the violin until he was certain the sepoy was dead. Then he returned, quaking, to the music-room to collect his sabre. But he was shaking so badly that he had to sit down and have a rest. "Thank heaven for that violin," he thought. "Still, I'd better not stay long with the sepoys attacking . . ." He thought he had better leave the pistol where it was; it was much too heavy to carry around if it was not going to work. He had scarcely made this decision when he looked up. The sepoy was standing there again.

Was he a spectre returning to haunt Fleury? No, unfortunately he was not. The sepoy was no phantasm . . . on the contrary, he looked more consistent than ever. He even had red welts around his throat where the violin strings had been choking him. Moreover, he was chuckling and making humorous observations to Fleury in Hindustani, his eyes gleaming as black as anthracite, pointing at his neck occasionally and shaking his head, as if over an unusually successful jest. Fleury made a dash for his sabre, but the sepoy was much nearer to it and picked it up, making as if to hand it to Fleury, and chuckling more loudly than ever. Fleury faltered backwards as the sepoy advanced, still making as if to offer him the sabre. Fleury tripped over something and sat down on the floor while the sepoy worked his shoulders a little to loosen himself up for a swipe. Fleury thought of jumping out of the window, but it was too high . . . besides, a thousand sepoys were waiting below. The object he had tripped over was the pistol; it was so heavy that it was all he could do to raise it. But when he pulled the trigger, it fired. Indeed, not just one barrel fired, but all fifteen; they were not supposed to, but that was what happened. He found himself confronted now by a midriff and a pair of legs; the wall behind the legs was draped in scarlet. The top half of the sepoy had vanished. So it seemed to Fleury in his excitement, anyway.

The Collector and half a dozen Sikhs were still managing to

hold the door into the drawing-room, but only just. [. . .]

The Collector had an unpleasant feeling that unless something unexpected happened he and the Sikhs would find themselves cut off . . . But just then something did happen.

Ever since Ford had pointed out the location of the sepoy magazine Harry had been unable to get it out of his mind. He had even fired a round shot in its direction with the long iron six-pounder at the normal maximum elevation, that is to say, five degrees; the brass six-pounder, of course, no longer consented to swallow round shot. The shot, as he had expected, had fallen short by somewhere between three and four hundred yards.

The difficulty was this: he wanted to increase the elevation to creep forward over those last 300 yards (he did not dare exceed the two-pound charge) but, as every gunner knows, increasing the elevation beyond five degrees can be a risky business; it is not the great number of rounds that destroys a cannon but the high elevation at which it is fired. A gun which at any elevation from point blank to five degrees could stand two hundred rounds without a strain, at thirty degrees would almost certainly burst before fifty rounds had been fired. And this iron six-pounder had already fired heaven only knew how many rounds before coming into Harry's hands at the banqueting hall. But when Fleury came back at last and told him how they were faring in the Residency, Harry knew he would have to take the risk.

The banqueting hall was now filled with ladies and children, refugees from the Residency. Before dawn Harry had set them to work collecting up any combustible material they could find; pieces of shattered furniture, empty ammunition cases, even books. Then, assisted by Ram and Mohammed, he had built a crude furnace of bricks on the verandah in which to heat up the shot. Now his heart was thumping as he turned the elevating screw past five degrees. Until he reached five degrees he had found that it turned easily, through long use . . . but now it became stiff and awkward. Yet Harry continued to turn.

When at last he was satisfied with the elevation he supervised the loading; a dry wad over the cartridge and then a damp one.

Then he ordered Ram to serve out the reddest shot he could find in the furnace, watched it loaded and, motioning the pensioners back, himself took the portfire and touched it to the vent. There was a crash. The cannon did not burst. A small, glowing disc swam calmly through the clear morning air trailing sparks. It climbed steeply for some moments and then hung, apparently motionless, like a miniature sun above the sepoy encampment. It dipped swiftly then towards the magazine and smashed through the flimsy, improvised roof. The flash that followed seemed to come not just from the magazine itself but from the whole width of the horizon. The trees on every side of the magazine bent away from it and were stripped of their leaves. A moment later the men who watched it explode from the verandah felt their ragged clothes begin to flap and flutter in the blast. The noise that came with it was heard fifty miles away.

The Collector did not know how the magazine had been blown up but he did not stop to wonder. While the sepoys hesitated, afraid that they were being attacked in the rear, he and the few surviving Sikhs made a dash for the trench and safety.

NADINE GORDIMER

NADINE GORDIMER

Nadine Gordimer was born in South Africa in 1923. Apart from being a joint winner of the Booker Prize in 1974 with *The Conservationist*, she has also won the James Tait Black Memorial Prize, the W. H. Smith Award, and French, Italian, American and German awards. Her nine novels include *Burger's Daughter*, *July's People* and *A Sport of Nature*; and her eight story collections include *A Soldier's Embrace* and *Something Out There*. Her latest publication is a collection of essays, *The Essential Gesture*.

Benoni – Son of Sorrow

How did I find out?

I was deceiving him.

November. I was on study leave – for two weeks before the exams pupils in the senior classes were allowed to stay home to prepare themselves. I would say I was going to study with a friend at the friend's house, and then I'd slip off to a cinema. Cinemas had been opened to us only a year or so; it was a double freedom I took: to bunk study and to sit in the maroon nylon velvet seat of a cinema in a suburb where whites live. My father was not well off but my parents wanted my sister and me to have a youth less stunted by the longings of an empty pocket than they had had, and my pocket money was more generous than their precarious position, at the time, warranted. So I was in the foyer waiting to get in to a five o'clock performance at one of the cinemas in a new complex and my father and that woman came out of the earlier performance in another.

There was my father; the moment we saw one another it was I who had discovered him, not he me. We stood there while other people crossed our line of vision. Then he came towards me with her in the dazed way people emerge from the dark of a cinema to daylight.

He said, "You remember Hannah, don't you?"

And she prompted with a twitching smile to draw my gaze from him – for I was concentrating on him the great rush of questions, answers, realisations, credulity and dismay which stiffened my cheeks and gave the sensation of cold water rising along my spine. She said, "Hannah Plowman, of course we know each other."

I mumbled, "Hello." He drew it from me; we were back again

in our little house in Benoni and I was being urged to overcome
the surly shyness of a six-year-old presented with an aunt or
cousin. "What are you going to see?" he said. While he spoke
to me he drew back as if I might smell her on him. I didn't know.
They managed to smile, almost laugh, almost make the exchange
commonplace. But it was so: the title of the film I had planned
to see was already banished from my mind, as this meeting
would have to be – ground away under my heel.

"The Bertolucci – an Italian film – it's very good," he said,
delicately avoiding the implications of the natural prefix "we
thought . . ." She nodded enthusiastically. "That's the one to
see, Will," he was saying. And the voice was an echo from
another world, another life, where he was my father, giving
me his usual measured, modest advice. Then he signalled a
go-along-and-enjoy-yourself gesture, she murmured politely,
and they left me as slowly as they had approached. I watched
their backs so I would believe it had really happened; that woman
with her bare pink bottle-calves and clumsy sandals below the
cotton outfit composed of a confusion of styles from different
peasant cultures, him in his one good jacket that I had taken to
the dry cleaners for him many times, holding the shape of his
shoulders, folded over my arm. Then I ran from the cinema
foyer, my vision confined straight ahead like a blinkered horse
so that I wouldn't see which way they were going, and I took a
bus home, home, home, where I shut myself up in my room,
safe among familiar school books.

Benoni – son of sorrow.

My father, who didn't have a university degree (unlike that
woman he admires so much) used to have the facility of picking
up knowledge that only intelligent people whose formal education
is limited, possess. He attracted fragments of information to
himself as I attracted my mother's pins to my horseshoe magnet.
One time he told me what the name of the town meant. I don't
know where he learnt it. He said it was Hebrew.

I was born in that town, his son. I think now that this sorrow
began when we left it. As long ago as that. Even before. When
he had to stop being a school teacher and his profession and his

community work were no longer each an extension of the other, something that made him whole. Our family whole. They found a job for him in an Indian wholesalers – the people on the committee against the removal of our people from their homes, which was now his community work, taking him all over the place, speaking on platforms and attending meetings outside the community of our streets, our area. He no longer had a profession, the profession he was so proud of serving; his profession had become the meetings, the speeches, the campaigns, the delegations to the authorities. The job – book-keeping or something of that kind he quickly taught himself – was not like teaching. It was a necessity that fed us and that was got through between taking the train to the city every morning and returning every evening. It had no place in our life. He did not bring it home, it was not present with us in the house as his being a teacher always had been. I was ten years old; he went away every day and came back; I never saw that warehouse at the other end of the train journey. "Men's and boys' clothing," he said: I had asked what was in it. Imagine him in cave after cave of shoes without feet, stacks and dangling strings of grey and brown felt hats, without heads or faces, he who had been surrounded by live children.

He used to read to us at night, my sister Baby and me, whenever there were no meetings. Baby didn't listen, she would go into the kitchen with her little radio. He had taught me to read when I was five years old but I still loved best to be read to by him. Sometimes I made him read to me from the book he himself was in the middle of, even though I didn't fully understand it. I learned new words – he would interrupt himself and explain, if I stopped him. When grown-up visitors asked the usual silly question put to children, Baby answered, depending on whether she was out to impress the visitor or be saucy, she would be "a doctor", "a beauty queen", and I said nothing. But he – my father – would say, "My son's going to be a writer". The only time I had spoken for myself everyone laughed. I had been taken to the circus at Christmas and what I wanted to be when I grew up was a clown. Baby called out (bright little madam, everyone dubbed her), "Because your feet's so big already!" My mother didn't want to see my feelings hurt and tried to change the derision to a rational objection. "But clowns are sad, Will," she said.

The faces they draw over their faces, the big down-turned mouth and the little vertical marks below and above the middle of each eye, that suggest tears. When he sat opposite me at supper that first night after the cinema, what face did he see on me? What face did he make me wear, from then on, to conceal him, what he was doing – my knowledge of it – from us: my mother, my sister, myself.

Perhaps if we had never left our area outside the small town it would never have happened? We would never have been there, he and I, at that cinema. She would never have found him, us – his blonde woman. I've thought of all the things that would have had to be avoided if I were not to have met my father at that cinema on an afternoon before the exams. I've lived them over in my mind because I did not know how to live now that I had met him, now that I had seen, not the movie I bunked swotting for, but what our own life is.

Although he worked in the city we had gone on living in our little house across the veld from the mining town for several years. My parents were paying off monthly instalments against the municipal loan with which they had bought it; my mother had her job running the crèche for Coloured Welfare. Except for him, everything was in its place. So we stayed where we were. The swing he had put up in the backyard when we were little, the kennel I'd helped him build for our Mickey, the dog he'd taken me to choose at the SPCA. While he was away with his committees and meetings at weekends my mother tried to do with us the things we all used to do together. And the last Sunday picnic before we left our home was in the winter. The last time; the end of winter. The veld had been fired to let the new growth come through; the sun burned off the night's frost as a cool zest on the smell of ashes. A black landscape with only our mountains, the mine dumps, yellow in the bright light. My mother spread a sheet of plastic under our rug over the sharp black stubble that puffed up like smoke under our feet and dirtied our socks. There were the things we liked to eat, *naartjies* whose brilliant orange skins Baby arranged in flower patterns on the blackness. Did he say, "My daughter's going to be an artist?" Because he was there. At that last picnic we had on our old patch of veld between the dumps, he was with us. He and I rambled off, I poking with a stick at every mound and hole for what treasures I did not know, and he showed me some, he discovered them for me; he always did. There was the skeleton of a fledgling caught by the fire; he said we could take it home and wire it together. Then he spied for me the cast of a *songololo* thick as my middle finger; I held up the empty coil of the worm and could see the sky through it at the end of its tiny tunnel. Ice-blue sky, yellow dumps, black veld, like the primary colours of a flag. Our burnt-out picnic. She would never have known where to find us, there.

But when she came to the house in Johannesburg, she had already found him. On her errands of justice and mercy she had visited the prison.

She is blonde, my father's woman. Of course. What else would she be? How else would he be caught, this man who has travelled so far from all the humble traps awaiting our kind, glue sniffing, drink, wife beating, loud-mouthed capering, obsequious bumming, and all the sophisticated traps of lackeyism, corruption, nepotism, which wait for men who take privilege at the expense of the lives of others, and of their own self respect. Self respect! It's been his religion, his godhead. It's never failed him, when he wanted to know what course to take next: his inner signpost, his touchstone. Do what will enable you to keep your self respect. That is the wisdom he has offered us – my sister and me. It came with the warm flow of assurance that floods you when you receive something to live by whose proof is there, in the person of the donor. If someone whose self respect has demanded and received so much from him – loss of the work he was dedicated to, transformation from contemplative privacy to public activity, speechifying, trial and incarceration, a prisoner of conscience – if *he* is to be caught, of course it's going to be in the most vulgar, shop-worn of sticky traps, fit for a dirty fly that comes into the kitchen to eat and shit at the same time on our food.

Of course she is blonde. The wet dreams I have, a schoolboy who's never slept with a woman, are blonde. It is an infection brought to us by the laws that have decided what we are, and what they are – the blonde ones. It turns out that all of us are carriers, as people may have in their bloodstream a disease which may not manifest itself in them but will be passed on; if he is a carrier, it has come to him from all that he has emancipated himself from so admirably – oh yes, I did, do admire my father. People talk of someone "coming down" with a fever; he's come down with this; to this.

Of course "we know each other". She entered our house when he was on trial and had been refused bail. I let her in. I opened the door, the schoolboy was the man of the house, for my mother and sister, now that he was not there. Each time, I prepared my expression, the way I would stand to confront the police come to search the house once again. But it was a blonde woman with the naked face and apologetic, presumptuous familiarity, in her smile, of people who come to help. It was her job; she was the representative of a human rights organisation sent to monitor the trial of my father and his colleagues and to assist them and their families. We didn't need groceries and my school fees were paid; my mother and Baby were both working and there was no rent owed because soon after we moved to the city my father had bought that house in what was called a "grey area" where people of our colour defied the law and settled among whites. (After the first family had done this, it was easy, since most of the white people wanted to sell and move out before property values dropped because of our presence.)

So we didn't need her. She sat on the edge of our sofa and drank tea and offered what is called moral support. She talked about the trial, the iniquity of the charges, the Defence's foreboding that the judge was a "bad judge", a secret member of the *Broederbond*, showing – but not showing off, she was all humility before our family's trouble – inside knowledge of the case she must have gathered from interviews with the lawyers and furtive exchanges in court with the accused themselves, during the judge's tea recess, across the barrier between the public gallery and the dock. She was so intense it seemed my quiet mother,

her hair groomed and elegant legs neatly crossed as if her husband were there to approve of the standard – the self respect – she kept up, was the one to supply support and encouragement.

Of course I know her. That broad pink expanse of face they have, where the features don't appear surely drawn as ours are, our dark lips, our abundant, glossy dark lashes and eyebrows, the shadows that give depth to the contour of our nostrils. Pinkish and white-downy – blurred; her unpainted lips, the embroidered blouse over some sort of shapeless, soft cushion (it dented when she moved) that must be her breasts, the long denim skirt with its guerrilla military pockets – couldn't she make up her mind whether she wanted to look as if she'd just come from a party or down from the Sierra Madre? Everything soft and undefined; except the eyes. Blue, of course. Not very large, and like dabs filled in with colour on an otherwise unfinished sketch.

And even if I hadn't known her, I could have put her together, like those composite drawings of wanted criminals you see in the papers, from an identikit. The schoolboy's wet dream. My father's woman. But I had no voluptuous fantasy that night. I woke up in the dark. It's hard for an adolescent boy to allow himself to weep; the sound is horrible. I suppose because it's his voice that's breaking.

STANLEY MIDDLETON

STANLEY MIDDLETON

Stanley Middleton was born in Nottingham in 1919, and went on to study at his home-town university. During the Second World War he served in the Armed Forces in England and the Far East. In the years after, he became a Visiting Fellow at Emmanuel College, Cambridge, taught English Language and Literature, and was Headmaster of English High Pavement College, Nottingham.

He has written twenty-eight novels including *Holiday*, joint winner of the Booker Prize in 1974. He is married with two daughters and five grandchildren.

The Lady of the Lake

Frost coated the boles and branches of trees, stiffened tumps of grass.

About us the fog hung low, unevenly, catching at the back of the throat, as the cold murderously stabbed the flesh round our noses. Edwin and I, both in short trousers, wrapped our scarves tighter and ran whirling our arms in paddle-boat circles to raise warmth, stopping now and then to drag up our stockings and laugh at the freezing, unaccustomed twilight of the November afternoon. The one football match woodenly progressed, trampling the pitch black-green in a white surround though the orange, clayey mud on the goal area was frozen hard still, nog-marks preserved from earlier, more temperate games. Odd grey elms with a clear lace-work of twigs could be seen in the middle distance while a few yards further on shapes were erratically erased. No far horizon existed; at best we could make out the hawthorn hedge floating behind the path at the top end of the football fields. Edwin and I felt we had the place to ourselves. It must have been Saturday and sixty years ago.

"Time we went home," I said. I was the younger, always first to call it a day.

We had only a vague idea of the hour of the afternoon; the single football match dragged on. Who the teams were we did not know; one or two spectators only stood muffled on the touchline, and silent. We had questioned a goal-keeper as he and we had peered out into the murk. His answer had been unintelligible, delivered below the collar of the misshapen, navy-blue overcoat he had struggled into against the cold. On the approach of opponents, easily forecast even in fog because the pitch sloped steeply away from him, he removed the garment, dropped it behind the goal-line (there was no net for an insignificant club-game), and widened his arms and legs against the approach of the enemy. Though a young man, in his early twenties I guess now, he had removed his dentures for the game, and that, the upturned collar and his constant watch eastwards left his speech incomprehensible.

"What did he say?" Ted was two years older than I, five years bolder. "Who are they?"

"Couldn't hear."

"Ask him again." The tone ripped piercingly.

"Who did you say?" I asked dutifully.

The keeper, struggling into his coat, muttered something but whether he named his team or cursed us I could not tell. We recognised anger in his voice.

"I hope they lose," Ted said. "Salmon-tin Rovers."

He was a boy of discrimination even then, and realised that the man was pinned between his posts. In later life he was to rise high in the Civil Service, to be knighted for the same powers of judgement.

"Sixteen-none." He completed the insult.

"Twenty-six," I backed him up.

"A hundred and twenty-six."

The keeper could bear no more.

"I'll thump yo' two." We heard that with pleasure and scuttled off as he lolloped towards us. A warning shout from downfield returned him to his line. We laughed, wheeling away, arms wide, Avros on patrol, tired of impudence.

We pushed our way through "Little Stinker", a copse so called from the "stinking nannies", wild garlic, which grew there, and on to "The Trenches". These were dug during the First World War for military manoeuvres, and must at this period have been no more than a dozen years old. Though they were now grassed over, they were still deep to small boys and made an admirable playground. This afternoon they were, I recall, frozen hard so that leaping into them was not without risk, and this and the bitter cold precluded our usual game of English and Germans which involved longer periods of lying about or stealthy creeping in between the short bursts of machine-gun noises and hand-to-hand fighting. War talk was common amongst us children, even to those born like me after the Armistice, and second-hand stories from boys whose fathers had served in France were listened to with awe. There were two or three returned soldiers in our street, but not on a single occasion did I hear one of them open his lips about his experiences. They walked, or cycled, or caught the tram to half-time jobs for heroes they were lucky to find. I, an old man now, remember the faces of these fathers, thin, haunted and young, and their eyes, which took in the same slate roofs, paving slabs and grained sash windows and front doors as mine, had seen for real what civilised governments could inflict on ordinary men.

Teddy and I jumped and shouted to keep warm.

We were scrambling out of one slightly wider breach when my companion, head above the parapet, pushed me back with a stiff left arm.

"What's that for?"

"A ghost." His whispering voice swooped and dipped on the vowel. He bared his teeth. "A g-g-g-ghost." He imitated the dialogue of the comic papers, each "g" pronounced deliberately separate.

We giggled, tumbling to our feet. Neither of us (our ages were nine and eleven) was anything except sceptical about supernatural manifestations, not counting, of course, those dilated upon in Sunday Schools, but our reading had begun to have an effect so that we were only too willing to devise book-based, ephemeral thrills as ingredients in our games. Reality added some weight. Dark figures stalked night streets in the long length of shadow between widely-spaced, fluttering gas lamps. The Northern Cemetery provided a tally of horrors, and every "jitty", a narrow passage between houses, its grisly saga.

"Where?" I asked, our heads up.

"Sssh."

Nothing. Frost-whitened sods. No sign of railway embankment, railings or sporadic trees. Only the float of streaked and shrouding fog. I peered out into no man's land as if I expected an apparition. Teddy had scared me and pleased me, both. I was grateful.

"There." His voice rasped.

A dark grey shape with a broad-brimmed hat tied down with a scarf moved between bushes. Now I saw it, now not. Not a token. It had glided away, as in the penny dreadfuls.

"It's a witch," I said.

"A spirit." He rolled his eyes, clutching his stomach.

I no longer play-acted as we crouched in the freezing afternoon, but the figure had gone. Bushes faded and reappeared. With a jerk on my legs Ted tumbled me into the trench bottom, on top of him. He threw me roughly aside and ran, whooping.

"It's after us. It'll get you. Radium." He slapped his backside, cowboy fashion.

We reached the football pitches breathless, hearts knocking, excited beyond measure, just in time to see our enemy's enemies hack one past the reach of the toothless keeper, now at the lower end. We clapped solemnly with gloved hands above our heads; we hadn't the breath to shout; he paid no attention to us as he cursed his full backs. The fog seemed to thicken; the far goal posts disappeared. Figures loomed and went without sense. Within minutes of an invisible kick-off the referee's whistle shrieked for full time. They had had enough. The goal-keeper picked up, donned and buttoned his coat earnestly, clumsily, but in so doing turned to grimace and bawl at us.

"I've warned yo' two."

"Gi' your mother her coat back," Teddy shouted.

The man shook his head as if baffled by the wit, and ambled silently, diagonally across the field after the retreating footballers. The fog seemed to veer.

"If they haven't put her in the work-'ouse," Ted called, encouraged by silence.

"Or the 'sylum." I topped him.

The keeper trotted on. He must have heard. He did not react. Two nil to us.

"Time we went home," I said again.

"One more round the lake," Teddy ordered. I was not keen, but he was already on the move, with me, meek as a mouse, hard at his heels. The "lake" was a misnomer we attached to two long fish ponds built on the course of a stream in the rich days of the squire. Now it was neglected, reed-fringed, dirty, the clay banks crumbling. We did not stop until we reached the further shore.

"Look at that ice," Ted said. "Thick as iron."

We searched the path for stones, hurling them at the black surface of the pond where they lifted a splinter before skidding on. Teddy now held a half brick.

"Watch this," he said, teetering on the edge and heaving the missile from his chest. It looped high and fell, marking the surface, not breaking it. It lay a yard or so from where it landed, ugly as the ice. "Told you," he said. "You could walk across that."

"*You* could, you mean."

He grinned. Neither of us would try. People had committed suicide here.

"What are you boys doing?"

We jumped out of our skin, turned, gaping.

The witch stood on the path by a bare bush. She wore a broad-brimmed hat with a scarf over the crown and under her chin, not unlike Hogarth's "Shrimp Girl", and a dun-coloured raincoat shorter than the black skirt which trailed almost to her ankles. In the sallow face the eyes were large and dark, the lips thin, bloodless, compressed. She wore ragged mittens.

"We're testing the thickness of the ice," Ted answered. He made it sound scientific, official.

The expression on her face did not change though when she spoke we saw her small, yellow teeth. She stood not six feet away from us, the raincoat belted.

"You be careful," she said. "Don't go on it whatever you do. It's dangerous. You could be drownded." She spoke without force, not looking at us any longer. "Are you brothers?"

"No. We've been watching the football."

The *non sequitur* had no impact; she stared away silently before the next soft, abrupt question.

"Do your mothers know you're here?"

"Yes. We come up every Sat'day." I left excuses to Ted.

"Go on home. They'll be worrying about you."

"Could you tell me the right time, please?" I asked.

"I don't know. Ha' past three, perhaps."

She breathed in as deeply as her shallow lungs allowed, and gently shook her head before moving, slipping away. In a second she was gone. Bush, fog and cold path remained.

"Oo-er," Ted ventured after a minute, keeping his spirits up. "I know who it is."

He rounded on me, expression superior. The worm did not often turn.

"Who?"

"Her name's Mrs Marriott." I made him wait; I did not often hold the upper hand. "She lives up Clarges or Nansen." I named streets.

"And how do you come to know her, Mr Clever-clogs Brian?"

"We met her on holiday when we went to Mablethorpe. Her mester works with your dad and mine." That would have been sixteen months ago; last August we spent our week in Yarmouth.

To meet people you recognised in some different environment was not unusual, but memorable. To see a known figure saunter-ing through Slab Square in town, or queuing for the Elite or the Hippodrome, or occupying a pew in a strange chapel for the Sunday School anniversary, was worth a mention at hearth or board. For one thing, they, and you, would be specially dressed for these festive occasions. At the seaside my father would don a grey trilby and sometimes an open-necked "cricket" shirt and sport white plimsolls which he blancoed each evening from a block ready for next morning on the beach. He'd as soon wear plimsolls at home as his work boots for "sacrament" at chapel. We made ourselves worth seeing. I had a blazer, not a jersey, and no socks or stockings. My mother invested herself in a flowered hat and a spotted kerchief. My father swung his walking stick as we took to the promenade.

We had not stopped on that afternoon to talk to the Marriotts though we let them know we had recognised them. Perhaps we "passed", as my father had it, "the time of day" or, more likely, more laconically, "we moved to them", that is, acknowledged them with a nod. My parents were not given to the larger social gestures. But the meeting on the front, and the naming of their names to my mother when they were out of earshot had been enough for sharp little eyes and ears to register.

"She didn't know you," Teddy derided. "I never heard of her." Dismissive.

"You have." We were a competitive pair.

"Who are you calling a liar?"

"Pound to a pinch," I said.

Teddy recognised confidence when he saw it. He looked me over with new respect.

"Go on," he ordered, magnanimously.

"Her son's in prison. He killed somebody."

"Luke Marriott?"

"Yes."

Six months back-street corners had been agog with the Luke Marriott case. The only son of decent parents, he was a teara-way, a drunk, a loud-mouth. He'd run wild as a teenager during the war with his dad away nearly four years in the army out East and his mother working in munitions. There had been more than one brush with the police. One night in "The Horseshoe" he'd picked a quarrel with another such as himself, Jackie Poyser, and in the course of fisticuffs after the landlord had thrown the pair out into the street he struck his opponent so violently (Marriott was strong, had graced, or disgraced the semi-professional ring), that he had broken the man's jaw in two places. Poyser, felled like an ox, cracked his head on a kerb stone, fracturing his skull, and he had died two days later in hospital. Luke escaped in panic, but was picked up within twenty-four hours in Derby and tried for murder. Front page headlines were black for a week. I remember the first time I went to the barber's (my father had trimmed my hair hitherto) where I had sat clutching my fourpence and listening to the five men on chairs ahead of me discuss the trial, the death. All claimed to know victim or accused. Phrases clanged as scissors snipped.

"Too bleddy handy wi' his dukes by 'alf."

"I know. I seen him fight that blackie up the 'Azel Street 'All. By God, there were some blood spilt in that ring."

"Bad tempered bastard 'e wor. And nivver sober after nine at night."

"I feel sorry for his mam, I do. Lovely woman. Lived next door to us."

They did not temper the wind of their eloquence to the as yet
unshorn lamb perched there drinking in every precious word,
but hugging my knowledge to myself.

My family sympathised with the father. Why such a decent,
steady, hard-working man should have had such a son was
beyond reason. My dad blamed the war. Poor Ernie Marriott
had taken it all very hard; he attended the trial, he visited his
son each weekend he could in Lincoln gaol after the verdict of
manslaughter, but he had failed himself. Never a cheerful man
before, he now became morose. His workmates could barely
prise a word out of him; he began to make bad errors; he took
days off; melancholy overcame him. Only his allotment provided
comfort, but that was not properly tended. Marriott had lost all
system and care; apples and pears rotted on the trees, but he
did not bother his head. My mother and father both called it
"tragic"; it was a new word to me, but I could guess.

Ted and I run-walking back home in the fog that Saturday
afternoon must have exchanged views about this, but nothing
remains. I can recall the goal-keeper and the woman with her
well-intentioned advice and sick, set face quite clearly. We did
not need her warning; we had more sense than to try our weight
on the ice, but she had perhaps spoken to us as to her son, out
of habit or in hope. She had made sufficient impression for me
to mention the meeting to my mother, who gave me her usual
half attention, but she remembered what I'd told her when at
the beginning of next week we heard that Ernest Marriott had
committed suicide.

On that foggy Saturday afternoon Marriott and his wife had
set out together, had spoken to a neighbour quite normally. Half
a mile short of the park he had turned off towards his allotment
and she in hat and scarf had gone walking on towards us and the
lake. He had locked himself in his hut; there was not a soul
about. At the very time she was warning us and staring at the
fog he had taken out his cut-throat razor to use on his wrists
and had let his blood drip away into a tin wash-tub he had pulled
into his shed. There was no note; presumably he had put the
razor into his pocket before they left home. When he hadn't
returned in the evening by eight o'clock, she'd put the raincoat

on again, the hat and scarf, and made for the allotment in the fog and there, breaking the window of the shed, had found him. She had then run nearly a mile to the police station.

She lived for another twenty years, I'm told, till after the Second War. Subdued, but sane, she kept the allotment going. I have heard nothing of Luke. She and her husband are buried together in the cemetery near to the grave of my parents and that of Ted's mother and father and brother.

Who paid for their gravestone and the one-word epitaph, "United", I do not know.

RUTH PRAWER JHABVALA

RUTH PRAWER JHABVALA

Ruth Prawer Jhabvala was born in Germany in 1927 of Polish parentage. She came to England as a refugee in 1939 and in 1951 married C. S. H. Jhabvala. She has written film scripts for James Ivory and Ismail Merchant, novels and short stories. The scripts include *Shakespeare Wallah*, *The Bostonians* (based on the novel by Henry James), *Heat and Dust*, (based on her own novel which won the 1975 Booker Prize), and *A Room With A View* (based on the novel by E. M. Forster). Her novels include *A New Dominion* and *Three Continents*; her short stories *Like Birds, Like Fishes* and *Out of India*.

After *Heat and Dust* in 1975, I didn't publish a novel until 1983. It was called *In Search of Love and Beauty* and was a departure from all my previous work. It is set in New York City and in upstate New York, and although India still features – I suppose it always will – it does so only in a minor way and no longer looms in, through, above and beneath all the characters and story. This book is for me a return beyond India and even beyond my English adolescence to scenes, characters, and landscapes which formed the essence of my earliest childhood. I'm here reprinting the very end of the book: not that anything very wonderful happens – on the contrary, one of the principal characters dies, two others are driving to their deaths, a fourth is involved in a petty homosexual quarrel. But that's how things turn out, or how I perceive them turning out, in the search for love and beauty. And then there's the snow falling through all these final scenes – snow of a quality I hadn't experienced since leaving Germany in the thirties, so that what happens here is wrapped in a white mist of nostalgia for a Europe I hadn't even known I missed until I met it again in America.

Extract from *In Search of Love and Beauty*

By the time Marietta came to collect her to take her to the Academy, Louise had so many packages that they had to call the doorman up to help carry them into the car. Before starting off, Marietta phoned Eric to tell him to have Regi ready, so that when they got to her apartment house, Eric had her down there sitting in the marble lobby, and he and Regi's doorman helped her get in the back of the car with Louise. Louise hugged and kissed her for her birthday and pointed out all the parcels and the enormous box holding the birthday cake; and Regi seemed well pleased – at any rate, she had no complaint. Her only anxiety was for the safety of the birthday cake, until Eric, up front with Marietta, took it on his lap and kept it sitting there the entire way.

The beginning of their journey was dull – getting out of the city, out of traffic jams, and through decaying areas full of empty littered sites and broken buildings with ornate fire-escapes. All the windows were boarded-up except here and there where a furniture-maker or other trader going out of business had put his stock on sale. It hadn't started snowing yet in the city, but the sky looked grim. People huddled in their coats and walked with their heads down against the wind which churned up litter from the pavements. The river was choppy and ugly brown, and the pleasure cruiser, which still stood on it, looked incongruous with its smart white paint and little coloured flags. But Louise, snug in the back of the heated car with Regi, looked out at everything with excitement and pleasure; and so did Eric who loved a ride.

Then they got out of the last thinning part of the city and began to strike out into suburbs and scenery. The highway turned into a parkway, and Marietta drove more and more smoothly over better roads: till at last for miles on end there were only trees and little woods to see, and sometimes a field rising to a hill with one house on top. Once they passed over a bridge and water stretching clear and far on either side; and shortly after that Louise leaned forward in her seat and then she cried: "Look, Regilein, *snow*!" But Regi was asleep and only grunted; what a pity – except that rest was always good – for Regi too had loved snow and winter sports.

As they drove further north, they came into a landscape that was already white, with snow hardening and still falling. Wherever there was water, it had turned to ice; and once Eric looked around at the two of them at the back to point out a little stream which, in falling down a precipice, had frozen mid-way into icicles. "Oh they're both asleep," he then said to Marietta. Louise heard him, and she wanted to cry out, "No, I'm not!"

But she didn't – was she really asleep? But how could that be, when she was so excited with the snow, and their outing to the Academy, and Regi's birthday. Too excited perhaps: she couldn't take that much any more, and it was exhaustion not sleep that had overcome her. She opened her eyes for a moment, but they fell shut again almost at once; and really perhaps she didn't need to keep them open – she could see within herself all the snow and all the ice she had ever experienced, and all the fun they had had in it. Louise had been a very good ice-skater: not fast and dazzling and swooping like some of the others, but slow and stately as a swan.

Bruno had proposed to her one day after he had watched her skate on the frozen pond of the Grünewald. She hadn't known he was there watching – she always went into a sort of trance when she was skating, she got so much enjoyment out of it. She was warm in her cloth coat with fur collar and hem, her head encased in a fur cap matching the muff that dangled from a string around her neck. She didn't keep her hands in it for she had her arms folded; she glided around on the ice with the same ease as she danced, not thinking of her feet at all. Her eyes were half-shut so that the bright crystal sunlight came to her dimly, and so did the voices of the other skaters. She didn't notice Bruno till it was time to leave when, with her easy rhythmic glide, she went to the edge of the pond; and there he was, holding out a gloved hand to help her. He sat beside her while she took off her skates; she was aware that he was looking and looking at her, and it made her face glow more. Bruno was also wearing a fur-collared coat, and there were drops of snow melting in it and in his moustache, which was the same colour as the fur.

He didn't propose to her there and then, but later in Schwamm's where he took her to warm her up with hot chocolate. Actually, she didn't need warming up – she was glowing, as always after skating – but his hands were icy cold, she noticed when he drew off his gloves. They sat at a round table in a corner by a magnificent gold-framed mirror in which she could see that he was still looking and looking at her. She was glad she was wearing a dress he hadn't seen before – a green and rust plaid wool with a bolero and a big black bow; it had been finished a few days earlier by the old lady who came to sew for Louise's mother every Wednesday. When the chocolate arrived, it was very hot, but Louise had a trick of sucking it out from under the cool cream on top. The only thing was, one had to watch out for a chocolate and froth moustache; so she was surreptitiously doing that in the mirror and wiping off a faint trace from her upper lip with her tongue when Bruno began to propose to her. She wanted to get back to her drink – she loved it so – but desisted, for she realised this was a very solemn moment; so she made a solemn face and he talked – oh so poetically! She was deeply stirred and thrilled and thought to herself it is for ever, for life, for the whole of life. And that seemed to her the most beautiful phrase she had ever thought: the whole of life.

Before going on to the Academy for Regi's birthday party, Mark drove to his house. He was surprised to see a sleek black saloon standing in his driveway. "Whose is that?" he asked Natasha who appeared on the front porch the moment she heard him drive up.

"Did Mother bring Grandma?" she asked.

"Yes, they must have arrived at Leo's . . . Why aren't you there? Why are you here?"

With these questions they got inside the hall. Now Mark heard voices muffled from behind the dining-room door; but before he could go in, she drew him away into the opposite room.

"What's going on?" Mark said. "Who's in there with him?"

"It's someone called Anthony," Natasha had at last to say.

"Oh I see." And Mark, looking grim, strode at once to the door.

Before he could open it, she had run in front of him and held on to the knob.

"Don't be ridiculous, Natasha."

Still holding on to the door, she began to plead: "Let's go – I was waiting for you to drive me there – Grandma must be waiting. They're all waiting, Mark. They must have brought the cake. Regi's cake. Let's go. They'll want to cut it." As she spoke, her eyes searched desperately over his face – as if she didn't know it already, better than any other in the world.

Instead of replying, he tried to prise her hand from the door. She knew she couldn't hold on much longer – he wasn't very strong, but at any rate stronger than she was – and she tightened her grasp on it and became more pleading: "Drive me there, Mark. I want to go. Please drive me." And then she let go of the handle and did something she had not done since their childhood: she flung her arms around his neck and clung to him, her face touching his. This contact, slight as it was – no more than a brushing of her cheek against his – filled her with a deep and poignant sensation; so that to feel him at the same instant recoil with what was at least distaste was correspondingly painful. But she willed herself to keep her hold on him; she even tightened her arms and said, "You're not to go in there."

Then he fought back. He loosened her arms from his neck and flung her aside. There was a look of wild fury on his face; and when he spoke, his voice was shrill: "I think you've gone crazy! You really are crazy! A crazy hysterical woman!" But it was he who sounded like one.

"No, don't!" she cried and again she tried to hold him, interposing herself between him and the door. And, "Don't," she said again in a quieter voice as she looked into his pale and twitching face; and what she meant now was not only "Don't go in there" but also "Don't look like that. Don't be like that." She wanted him calm, manly, himself.

But at that moment to be himself was to get rid of her and go into the other room and deal with whatever was going on there. "Get out of the way," he said, and he didn't scruple now to push her roughly. At that all the fight went out of her. She knew she didn't have a chance. She moved aside, and he opened the door. She followed him into the hallway, and as he went towards the dining room, she went to the front door to let herself out. She didn't want to hear anything of what was going to happen.

However, just before opening the door to the dining room, he stopped short and looked after her and had second thoughts.

He called to her, and when she didn't turn around, he went to her.

"I won't be long," he said. "I'll take you in a moment. If you'll just be patient and wait."

She had turned her face aside so he plucked at her hair as if he were ringing a bell; it was what he sometimes did when he wanted to attract her attention. But now she put up her hand and brushed his aside. "Hey!" he said. "What's with you?" And he looked into her face which she tried to avert from him so that he wouldn't see how sad she was.

But he knew that very well; he knew it exactly. He stood there, torn between her and what was going on behind the dining room door: but then a voice came raised from out of there, and at that he could not be held a moment longer. He murmured, "We'll talk later" – shamefacedly perhaps, but it was with determination that he left her and went straight into the dining room and let her go out of the house.

The dining room: the way Mark had furnished it was almost an exact replica of what his paternal grandmother's had been. Yet only the candelabra, some of the Georgian silver, and the carving-set on the sideboard had come to him from her, while the rest he had bought at auctions and from antique dealers. On the other hand, the portraits on the walls really were his ancestors – the Senator, the Abolitionist, the sweet-faced General's wife who had died in childbirth – but they had been so carefully cleaned, so tastefully restored that they looked as impersonal as the rest of the furniture and might equally well have been bought in antique shops.

Seated at the table where Mark planned to give his dinner parties – he was getting an appropriate set of dishes together – were Kent and Anthony. They were side by side, and Anthony had laid his hand on Kent's. He left it there when Mark came in – perhaps in challenge: at any rate the way he looked up at Mark was defiant.

Kent said in his growling, deep voice, "I didn't ask him to come here."

"But he *is* here," Mark said.

"I didn't ask him," Kent said again. He looked down at

Anthony's hand on his and seemed surprised to see it there; and only then did he withdraw his from underneath.

"I've come to take him away with me," Anthony said.

"Oh yes? And what does he say about that?"

Kent didn't have anything to say. He stared ahead of him into horizons of his own, frowning, absenting himself from the scene.

Mark saw that he and Anthony were expected to fight it out between them. He was prepared to do that. He stood by the sideboard (inlaid with matching veneers) and Anthony came to join him there. They faced each other. Trim and fair, with careful haircuts and elegant casual suits, they looked so much alike that they might have been brothers. But there was this difference – that under his boyish haircut and over his young-man's suit, Anthony's face was strained and old. Looking at him, Mark might have been looking at his own face twenty years later; but not yet, not now.

Anthony said, "He wants to come and live with me. We've been talking about it. You can ask him."

Kent had his back to them and gave no one any help. He sat there stolidly and now he even supported his elbows on the table and held his hands over his ears.

"I don't think he wants to at all," Mark said. "If he did, I wouldn't try and stop him."

"You can't stop him."

They kept on glaring at each other. Mark felt at an advantage – in years, strength, everything. He wasn't even sure that he urgently wanted or needed Kent, but he was certainly determined that no one was going to take him away.

"Do you want to go, Kent?" he asked.

They both knew there wasn't going to be any answer, so instead Anthony spoke. He said, "Leave him out of this. I'm telling you: he wants to go with me." His voice rose to a falsetto: "Do you think you own him? Do you think you bought him, with this house, as part of the furniture?" Anthony's mouth twitched, so did his hands; Mark could have felt sorry for him – perhaps he even did, especially as he knew so exactly how he was feeling.

"Listen," Mark said. "You'd better drive yourself home now.

They said on the radio there's going to be a very bad snowstorm. I wouldn't like anything bad to happen to you driving back by yourself."

Anthony replied with bravado: "I'm not driving back by myself."

This was followed by too long a silence. When Anthony spoke next, the bravado had gone out of him. "Kent?" he said in a trembly voice, turning in that direction.

Kent let Mark speak for him – and Mark was glad to do so. He felt triumphant and superior, and couldn't help showing it on his face; and he said, calmly: "You must realise yourself that it was not a good idea to come here."

Anthony did something entirely unexpected: he snatched one of the silver-handled carving knives out of the stand – the same Mark's Aunt Mary had used on the Thanksgiving turkey – and he directed it towards Mark's heart. Now Anthony knew how to wield a carving knife – he could cut up roast chickens expertly – but not how to plunge it into other people's hearts. Or perhaps at the last moment caution overcame his rage. He got as far as Mark's pale blue Kashmir sweater and slit into that, crying, "I'll kill you!" And with that cry the knife clattered to the floor, and both Mark and Anthony stared down at it.

Mark stooped to retrieve it and, in his tidy way, to replace it on the stand. He touched the tear in his sweater, and Anthony, watching him do that, said, "Good God."

"Yes," Mark agreed.

Anthony straightened the necktie under his fiercely working Adam's apple. He said, "I guess I'm sorry," in a strangled voice.

"So you ought to be," Mark said. "It was quite a favourite sweater."

He managed to smile, and so, with more effort, did Anthony. But Kent was devastated – he had buried his head in his arms laid on the table. The other two had to comfort him, each placing a hand on one of his huge shoulders, now shaking with sobs. He was still very young, only at the beginning of his career, and knew nothing of what could sometimes happen among people with very strong feelings.

About these feelings: Leo had once likened them to the voices of the great *castrati*, in which a man's vigour was made to give body to a woman's nervous delicacy. Unhuman voices, Leo called them; unnatural hybrids. "All the same," Mark had replied, "no one ever said they weren't beautiful."

When they arrived at the Academy, Louise was so excited that she embraced everyone, even people she didn't know. "Where's Natasha?" she asked. Leo looked around: "Yes, where is she?" No one knew. Louise wouldn't allow Eric to take off Regi's hat and coat because she wanted to take her out again at once to show her the Academy grounds. "You don't come," she told Leo. "I don't want you with a cold." He didn't hear her. He said: "Where's Stephanie?"

Louise had taken Regi's arm and she carefully descended the steps out into the garden with her. When Eric tried to help, she wouldn't let him; she said they could manage perfectly well, this wasn't the first time she and Regi had been out in the snow together. "Is it darling?" she said, squeezing Regi's fur sleeve. But Regi said, "When are we going to open my presents?"

Louise took her to the sunken garden. Marietta and Eric and a few students came up behind them, in case they needed help. But the two old ladies seemed to be managing quite well on their own, clinging to each other as they tripped over the hardened snow. Both of them tall and completely encased in fur coats and fur hats, they looked like two prehistoric animals – cumbersome yet graceful because so perfectly adapted to their environment. Their high-heeled suede boots made the first tracks in the virginal snow of the sunken garden. Louise led Regi to the edge of the fountain basin. She showed her the stone nymph, whose curves were now packed with snow; icicles had formed at the stone nipple from which in the summer she pressed a fountain. "Brrrr," Louise playfully shuddered at Regi. "Aren't you glad you've got your mink?"

"When are we going to cut the cake?"

The water in the basin had frozen solid – "Just nice for skating," Louise said; and still in her playful mood, she stuck out one toe towards the ice and the tip of her tongue emerged between her lips in pleasant anticipation.

But Regi didn't want to go skating, she wanted to go in where her cake and presents were. She said crossly, in German, "Let me go, you stupid goose": and she jerked her arm free – so that Louise, one foot extended towards the ice, the other on the slippery surface of the snow, lost her balance and fell, striking the rim of the basin.

The others rushed forward to help her up. She was hurt but no one suspected how badly – except Eric who had seen old ladies slip and fall more than once before, on the ballroom floors round which he had led them in the fox-trot, the peabody, and the old-fashioned waltz. They usually broke a hip and had to be taken away in the ambulance; once one of them had died before they could even call the ambulance. Some of them died in hospital, but others came out again and hobbled around a while longer. However, none of them ever came back to dance again.

After Mark had gone to join the others in the dining room, Natasha didn't want to stay in the house with them. She walked down the hill to wait for him in Jeff's cottage. She hoped he wouldn't be long because, with the wood stove gone out, it was cold in there. She huddled in the rubbish dump armchair, with her hands in the pockets of her coat; her breath came in vapours. The cold outside seemed to be taking over the deserted cottage as if it were a dead tree with a hollow trunk.

She was relieved when she heard a car and got up to lift the latch from the door. But it was Leo who rushed in – like a wild man, wearing nothing over his monk's robe, his silver ornament swinging. He didn't say anything but his eyes rolled around the room, and when all he saw was her, he said, "Where have they gone?"

Natasha couldn't tell him; she really didn't know. She said, "Has Grandma come?"

He seized her arm as if she were unwilling to go with him; though at the same moment she was saying, "Take me back to the Academy." He hustled her into his car. She was surprised to see that it was his own car – a very small red sports model which he had had for thirty years. His followers wouldn't let him drive it any more because it was so old and also because he was such a mad, erratic driver. And he drove madly now, with Natasha beside him: the tiny car lurched and groaned as he wildly, doggedly drove it over the slippery road; it heaved and thumped and boiled. Natasha, who had never learned to drive, didn't realise how dangerous it all was. Instead she was glad to be getting back to the Academy so fast, to where Louise and Marietta were waiting with Regi and the birthday cake.

But after a time she realised that he was driving in the wrong direction, not towards but away from the Academy. It took some time longer before she plucked up courage to point this out to him. It was doubtful whether he heard her. He was hunched over the wheel, wheezing as loudly as the old car, his heavy, sack-like body lurching every time the car lurched from one side of the road to the other. Natasha said it again: "Leo, we're going the wrong way."

He was muttering; he was saying, "I'm going to find her. We'll find her." It was crazy. He looked and sounded crazy. His face was inflamed, his nose swollen, tears were coming out of his eyes and falling down his cheeks on to the steering wheel. He was making sobbing sounds like a baby or a very old man. Natasha was awestruck: "He really loves her," she thought. At the same time this thought depressed her, for it seemed to her that there just wasn't enough love to go round and never would be – not here, not now – with everyone needing such an awful lot of it.

Although it was still afternoon, dusk was falling – imperceptibly, for all day the clouds had not cleared and there was no sun to set, only sky and white earth to fade together into a colourless twilight. This was relieved by one single star which had appeared and glowed dimly in mid-air. It didn't occur to Leo to turn on the lights – he was too sunk in other thoughts that made him mutter as he lurched and drove and wept. It seemed to Natasha that the pale twilight, the fading earth were swallowing them up, sucking them in, as into water or clouds. Nevertheless, she was glad to be there with him: not that she could do anything as, blinded with tears, he drove them further into snow and mist, but at least so he wasn't alone.

*   *   *

They carried Louise into the den and laid her on the leather couch. She sighed when they did that – probably with pain, but perhaps also because she felt satisfied to be there in that hot, close room full of Leo's cigar smell. Regi's cake had been taken out of the box and placed on the round table in the centre where it shone pink and festive.

Regi wanted the candles lit. There were four of those – for herself, Louise always had the full amount (on her last birthday, her cake had blazed resplendently with eighty-four candles); but for Regi she left out the first digit. When everyone ignored her, Regi became more plaintive and louder – until she penetrated whatever it was that made Louise keep her eyes shut. Anyway, Louise opened them and said, "Let her", so then Eric lit the four candles. They made a very pretty sight, and Regi laughed and clapped her hands, and Louise too seemed to smile as she shut her eyes again.

But the very next second something happened within her – it was as if a stone broke through a vein and lodged itself inside her lungs: filling her with a sensation surpassing all others, a pain so sharp that it became transporting. She cried out, though just once and not very loudly, and only Marietta heard her. "I'm coming!" was what Marietta heard – as she had heard her mother exclaim once before, years and years ago when she had watched her and Leo from behind the screen. And Marietta wondered now as she had wondered then – what's she mean? Where's she coming? Where's she going?

Regi gathered herself together to blow her four candles out, but although she tried very hard, she only managed three and one remained. Nevertheless, Eric praised her for her effort, and then he said, "Now let's try again – one more time, okay?" So Regi took another deep breath and blew the last one out, terribly pleased with herself.

DAVID STOREY

DAVID STOREY

David Storey was born in 1933, was married in 1956 and has
two sons and two daughters. He studied at the Slade School of
Fine Art in London and is a Fellow of University College,
London. He has written a number of plays which include *The
Contractor, Home, The Changing Room, Life Class , Early Days,*
and *The March on Russia.* Apart from winning the Booker
Prize in 1976 with *Saville* he has won the John Llewellyn Rhys
Memorial Prize and the Geoffrey Faber Memorial Prize as well
as the Somerset Maugham Award. His novels include *This
Sporting Life, Flight into Camden, Radcliffe, Pasmore* and *A
Prodigal Child.*

Extract from *Saville*

The winter passed. At Easter a party from the school went
away on holiday. They stayed in a guest house at the foot of a
mountain. One evening Colin and Stafford went out to a nearby
village. A hump-backed bridge looked out over a lake. From a
row of small houses behind them came the sound of singing.

Stafford paused.

Three or four men and women were singing what sounded,
from this distance, like a wordless song. No other sound came
from the village; columns of smoke drifted up against the light-
ness of the sky, the dark shapes of the houses strewn out like
boulders at the foot of the mountain. At the peak of the mountain,
overlooking the village and the bright expanse of lake beyond,
snow glistened in the moonlight.

Stafford leant against the parapet of the bridge. He'd lit a
cigarette on the way down from the hotel and now, his head
back, his arms crooked on the stone parapet behind, he blew
out a stream of smoke, half smiling.

"What do you think?" he said. "They've put me down for
Oxford."

"Who?" he said.

"Gannen. I'm going to have special coaching in Latin. They've
put me down for an Exhibition."

"Don't you think it's worth it?" he said.

Stafford shook his head. "What do you do with life, do you
think?"

Perhaps he hadn't heard the singing, for he stubbed out the
cigarette, leaning over the parapet and dropping it into the

darkness of the stream below: odd, almost luminescent crests of foam shone up, here and there, from the deepest shadows. Stafford kicked the toe of his shoe against the stone.

"It seems worth going for, I suppose," he said.

Stafford shrugged. He looked up at the cold, cloudless depth of sky, glanced, almost with a look of irritation, towards the moon, and added, "I don't think, really, it's worth all that effort. What really is? Have you any idea?"

"No."

"If you did, in any case, you'd never tell me. You're such an eager beaver. I suppose, with you, getting a job, a house, a car, a wife, and all that sort of stuff, is all that matters."

"No," he said and turned away.

Perhaps Stafford, aware of the singing, had assumed it to come from a wireless. With the same look of irritation he'd given the moon, he glanced up now towards the houses. A door had opened somewhere followed immediately by the barking of a dog.

"What a dead and alive hole this really is. I don't suppose there's a pub or anything," he said, moving slowly from the wall, still kicking his toe and, his hands in his pockets, setting off towards the village. "I mean, what are we when it comes down to it?" he added. "A piece of something whirling through nothing and getting," he went on, "as far as I can see, nowhere at all." He waited for Colin to catch him up. "In a thousand million years the sun'll burn up the earth, and all that everybody's ever done or thought or felt'll go up in a cloud of smoke." He laughed. "Not that we'll be here to see it. Yet metaphorically one sees it. I feel it all the time as a matter of fact." He walked on in the darkness of the road, still kicking his toe, the sound echoing from the walls of the houses on either side. "Everything's so easy for you," he added. "You've come from nowhere: they've put the carrot of education in front of you and you go at it like a maddened bull. I couldn't do half the work you put into it, you know. I can see," he went on more slowly, "what lies the other side."

"What does lie the other side?" Colin said, walking beside him now, his hands in his pockets.

"Nothing, old boy," Stafford said, and laughed. "Take away

the carrot, and there really isn't anything at all. It's only someone like you, crawling out of the mud, that really believes in it. Once you've got it, you'll see. You'll sit down and begin to wonder: 'Is that really all it is?'" He laughed again, glancing across at him from the darkness.

They'd come out from between the houses and emerged on a stone embankment which, for a few yards, ran along the edge of the lake.

"I mean, what does Hepworth tell us about these mountains? This lake, you know, and this U-shaped valley. They were formed by ice ten thousand years ago. Here's a few houses put down at the side: a few people live in them, go through God knows what privations, misery, exaltations, and in another ten thousand years another sheet of ice comes down and wipes it all away. That, or an atom bomb. So what's the point of suffering or enduring anything at all?"

Colin waited. Beneath them, with a dull, almost leaden sound, the lake lapped against the stone. It washed up in little waves over a bed of pebbles, the white foam glistening in the light.

"I suppose you believe in a Divine Presence and all the rest of the propaganda," Stafford said. He stooped to gaze down at the water as if, for a moment, he'd suddenly forgotten anyone else was there.

"I don't know what I believe in," Colin said.

"Material progress, backed by a modicum of religious superstition. I can read it in your features," Stafford said. "You even play football as if you meant it. And if there's anything more futile than playing sport I've yet to see it. Honestly, at times I just want to lie down and laugh."

"I suppose it's more touching than anything else."

"Touching?" Stafford glanced across at him and shook his head.

"If everything is meaningless, that, nevertheless, we still ascribe some meaning to it."

Stafford laughed. He flung back his head. His hair, caught by the moon, glistened suddenly in a halo of light. "Touching? I call it pathetic."

He took out another cigarette, lit it, tossed the flaming match into the lake, glanced round him with a shiver and added, "We better get back. There's nowhere to go. That's symptomatic, in a curious way, of everything I've said." Yet later, lying in his bed, Hopkins snoring and Walker half whining in sleep in their beds across the room, he had added, "Do you see some purpose in it at all, then, Colin?"

He could see Stafford lying on his back, his head couched in his hands. The moonlight penetrated in a faint, cold glow through the thin material of the curtains.

"I've never really looked for one," he said.

"You're an unthinking animal, are you?" Stafford half turned his head, yet more to hear the answer than to look across.

"No," he said.

"Are you frightened of admitting you believe in a Divine Presence?" Stafford said.

"No," he said.

"You do admit it, then?"

Colin paused. He gazed over at Stafford whose head, though not turned fully towards him, was still inclined in his direction.

"It's only when everything has lost its meaning that its meaning finally becomes clear," he said.

"Does it?" Stafford gazed across at him now quite fiercely.

"For instance, I enjoy coming here," he said.

"Oh, I enjoy coming here," Stafford said. "I suppose I enjoy coming here. I haven't really thought about it. Not to the degree that you have." He waited. "If there isn't a Divine Presence don't you think it's all a really terrible joke? I mean, if the world's going to end as all worlds do, as an exploding mass of sunburnt dust, what's the purpose in anything at all? It's like a man taking infinite pains over his own funeral. I can't see the point of it. I mean, if God's going to allow the world to vanish, as all worlds do, what's the point of putting us in it in the first place? To give him a clap, do you think? I mean do you think, really, He's looking for applause? Or that He isn't actually there at all; at least, not in any form that could be defined outside the realms of a chemical reaction?"

Hopkins groaned in his sleep; Walker whined freshly through his congested nose.

"Just look at Hoppy. Just listen to him. Do you think there's a divine purpose then in that?"

Yet, perhaps because of the freshness of the walk, of the air outside, or because of the vague, persuasive murmur of Stafford's voice, he felt himself being drawn downwards into sleep: he opened his eyes briefly, saw Stafford, silent now, with his head couched once more in his hands, gazing with wide eyes towards the ceiling, then remembered nothing more until he heard the calls of Hopkins and Walker across the room, and the sound of a gong from the hall downstairs.

Below them, when they reached the snowline, lay a vast area of undulating heath and coniferous woodland, interspersed with the cold, metallic sheen of several narrow lakes: a waterfall tumbled immediately below them to the village, and it was here, on the way up, that Stafford had paused and looking round at Colin, still casual, half smiling, had said, "Do you ascribe to it a divine purpose, or are we ants, mechanistic functions, crawling on an arbitrarily eroded piece of rock?" not waiting for an answer but glancing up, past the head of the corrie lake to where the flattened, cone-shaped peak of the mountain faded away into a mass of swiftly-moving cloud. Gannen, booted, plus-foured, with a walking stick and a small haversack on his back, had glanced behind him. "Do I hear a sceptic amongst the ranks?"

Several boys at the front had turned.

"Was that your comment, Stafford," he added, "on the scene below?"

"It was merely a speculation, prompted by the view, sir," Stafford said.

"Far be it from me to ascribe a divine purpose to anything, particularly when I examine the sea of disingenuous faces I see below me at the present," Gannen said. "Nevertheless, examining the terrain beyond, even I, historian that I am, and acquainted with all the more perfidious traits of man, would confess to a feeling of uplift, of exhilaration, and might even ascribe to it an extra-terrestrial significance. After all, we are the end products, as Mr Macready, a biologist, will tell us, of several million years of evolution, and who is to say, standing at the threshold of human existence, what significance we might ascribe to it? In years to come humanity might stretch out its tentacles to the moon, or, conceivably, beyond the sun, to other galaxies perhaps. We stand today near the summit of a mountain: who can say where a man might stand in, for the sake of argument, another thousand years? God, as the philosopher might say, Stafford, is a state of becoming, and we, as the psychologists might say, are the elements of his consciousness."

Stafford smiled; he looked past Gannen and the boys strung out below him on the path to where the small, grey-haired figure of Hepworth was climbing up the slope towards them with the slower group.

"Stafford, of course, would have no time either for the philosopher or the psychologist," Gannen said. "He is one of the modern school, the sceptics, who see humanity as merely the fortuitous outcome of biological determinism. Like ants, I believe was the phrase, crawling on an arbitrarily eroded piece of rock. Hopkins, of course, doesn't care what we are, nor, no doubt, does Walker, as long as he can get his bottom at the earliest opportunity to the seat of a chair and hands and feet warmed up in front of a fire."

Macready had taken a small bottle from his haversack and was tasting its contents. He tossed back his head, closed his eyes, then, replacing the bottle, glanced up with blank incomprehension at the peak before them.

It was late in the afternoon by the time they got back to the hotel. Rain was falling. Platt was standing in the doorway with the other boys who had stayed below, waving to Gannen as he appeared in the drive and calling, "We were just thinking of coming to look for you."

"Oh, just a routine climb, Platty," Gannen said, removing his haversack and looking round at the exhausted boys. "Apart from nearly going over the edge on one occasion, the afternoon you might say has passed without incident. Though," he added, "we had to call on Stafford to invoke a divine blessing on our behalf. The fact of the matter was, for half an hour after we left the summit – from which, incidentally, we saw nothing at all – Mac and I were lost. If the sun hadn't come out, very briefly, in what

Stafford might call a fit of arbitrary intervention, I don't think we'd be back at all."

And later, when the corridors of the hotel were full of steam from the baths, Stafford, flushed with the heat of the water, and with a towel around him, had come into the room and said, "I never thought Gannen was a sentimentalist until today. I don't think I'll get through history. It takes credibility from anything he says," lying on the bed, feeling in his jacket for his cigarettes, then adding, "Honestly, with a man like that, what chance have I got of an Exhibition?"

PAUL SCOTT

PAUL SCOTT

Paul Scott was born in 1920 in London, and died in 1977 within
a few months of winning the Booker Prize for *Staying On*. Cancer
had been diagnosed while he was teaching at the University of
Tulsa and he was too ill to return to receive the Prize. His
post-Army career in India started when he became Company
Secretary to Falcon Press, a small publisher; and continued
during the fifties when he worked at David Higham, the literary
agents. His first novel, *Johnnie Sahib*, appeared in 1952, but
real success only came with the *Raj Quartet* which he completed
in 1975.

Hilary Spurling writes:

Paul Scott wrote the first draft of his Cinderella story, *After the Funeral*, in the autumn of 1976, just over a year before he died. Re-working a fairy-story was one of the assignments he set his creative writing class as a visiting professor at the University of Tulsa, Oklahoma, that autumn semester. Scott was fifty-six. He had never taught before, and his students had never met anyone like him. He had just finished writing *Staying On* (page proofs arrived for correction while he was at Tulsa). The book was a kind of footnote or pendant to the *Raj Quartet*, itself completed the year before on publication of the fourth and final novel in a sequence begun ten years earlier with *The Jewel in the Crown*. The Quartet had brought its author no profit, financially speaking, nor any great critical acclaim in literary quarters. The first serious and sustained attempt to recognise his achievement had come from an historian, Max Beloff, writing earlier that year in *Encounter*.

The Quartet had cost Scott something like twenty years preparation as well as a decade to write. He was taking stock that autumn at Tulsa: looking back over his life and writing career, assessing in both personal and professional terms the race he had run, the prizes he had aimed at, and the price he had paid. He told his students that they must write what they knew, and that in anything they wrote they must find what he called the central emotional knock. Scott was sitting on the floor in his shabby student apartment when he said this, and he knocked with his knuckles on the ground beside him.

"Cinderella knocked for him." said one of his students. "He was getting at that central knock."

He brought the story back with him to London at Christmas,

took it out again in the spring, and rewrote it for publication in a limited edition with drawings by his younger daughter, Sally Scott, who was a professional illustrator. They worked on it intermittently together throughout what turned out to be the last year of his life. Scott returned to Tulsa for a second semester in the autumn of 1977. Word had passed round the campus that he was coming: his old students chartered a bus, drove out to the airport and clapped as he came off the plane. New ones flocked to enrol for his class. But he was already seriously ill, so depleted and drained that before the term was half over he was in hospital, still continuing to set class assignments and correct them from his bed.

He was operated on in October and found to have terminal cancer. By this time he knew that *Staying On* was on the Booker shortlist but, when the judges reached their decision in November, he was too weak to travel. His elder daughter Carol, who had flown out to be with him, flew back to receive the prize in his place. The student who had noted what Cinderella meant to him dropped in the day after Thanksgiving, the night of the Booker prize-giving, and found him alone in his apartment. Scott asked her what the time was. "It was about two o'clock. 'They will all be sitting down to dinner right now', he said. It struck me then how like that story it was."

Scott's *After the Funeral* is on one level a parable of the writer, the artist who feels shut out or cold-shouldered by the rest of the world, the dreamer whose ball takes place in his or her head. "The tale is like a looking-glass," he wrote, "in which you see yourself if you gaze into it long enough." Scott remained in some sense an outsider all his life. It might be argued that the long perspective he took in the *Raj Quartet*, the scope and sweep of his view of the end of empire, would only have been possible for someone who had never really belonged to the British social, political or for that matter literary establishment.

Scott died on 1 March 1978. His Cinderella story was published the year after. "I picked the right title in *After the Funeral*, didn't I?" he had said to his publisher on his deathbed.

Extract from *After the Funeral*

After the last funeral guest had gone she climbed the tower to her room and took off the white dress her dead mother's sister had sent her to enable her to be decently clothed for the occasion.

In this country white was the colour of both birth and death but after their baptism girls as young as Cinderella did not expect to wear it again until they were older. She was but fifteen. Her mother was already four days gone from the world. She folded the dress with sprigs of lavender and thyme which were moistened by one or two of the tears she had not shed at the funeral. She placed the dress carefully inside the white linen bag the carrier had brought it in and would call for tomorrow, with his horse and cart, to return to its sender who lived very far away and who was her godmother as well as her aunt and who had woven her christening shawl but whom she did not recall ever seeing except in dreams.

She put on her working dress, which was black, the colour in that country of life and living, and ran down the winding stone staircase which was as cold as a tomb, and entered the kitchen. She cleared the dishes, washed up, wound the clock and stoked the fire.

During her mother's long illness the kitchen had become her home. Although she was the youngest of three sisters she had developed a passionate sense of duty to it, even of possessiveness toward it: perhaps because she had had to. She mulled some wine for her stricken father, now asleep upstairs but likely to wake; she gathered together the best of what was left of the as yet unpaid-for funeral meats and set them neatly on plates, and the plates on trays, for her always hungry elder sisters who were upstairs with their feet up, soothing their headaches. Their best outdoor shoes, muddy from the graveyard, were by the fireside and had as yet to be cleaned. She looked at her own shoes, the only pair she had which were also set by. The graveyard mud did not seem to have clung to them. She thought: "Perhaps I step more lightly than they do? Is this a fault or virtue in me?"

She scattered the crumbs of the leftovers near the mousehole. The mice were all in mourning too, for there was not one of them who ever came out of the hole that was not white.

This was a long time ago. It is an old tale but somewhere in it there is the magic of a persistent wish, as old as earth but ever present. The tale is like a looking-glass in which you see yourself if you gaze into it long enough.

There was a mottled mirror on the wall above the kitchen fireplace, next to the clock that had to be wound every day but had lost its chime. In this glass Cinderella was sometimes startled to find an image of herself looking more beautiful than she felt could be true or thought likely. And there had been a day, when her mother was still alive, but ill, and Cinderella was doing the chores, when she caught her own eye in the glass and suddenly wept: wept for her mother who she guessed was dying but also for her sisters who were idle and ugly; and then for her father whom she loved but knew was vain and ambitious but weak and never likely to succeed, but who worked hard at keeping up appearances. And then she wept for herself; because oneself is the person one always really weeps for in the end.

Her father was a baron. The kitchen was in the basement of a castle and had once been staffed by cooks and scullions, stewards and pantrymaids. She scarcely remembered what it had been like then but had a dim recollection of it being brightly lit by lanterns and candles and tapers and filled with plump laughing people arranging meals for many guests. Since then, parts of it had become areas of darkness that frightened her, so that sweeping them she sometimes shut her eyes and was glad when, her work finished, she could sit by the welcoming fire and stir the iron cauldron in which the soup for supper was gently simmering, or burnish the few remaining copper pans that hung in the fireplace and became alive with all the images and reflections of the flames.

"The house one lives in must always have a warm heart," her mother had said. For Cinderella it was still here, in the kitchen.

*   *   *

With the exception of the baron's room which had been kept up because it was there that he faced his creditors, standing proudly in spite of his gouty leg, the rest of the castle was bleak; most of its rooms empty. One by one the servants had gone and the beautiful ornaments, valuable furniture and rich carpets had also gone, to pay his debts. Chill winds came through the broken panes of the windows and Cinderella's sisters who, she suspected, had no chance of marriage except to men who would be too old and ill-favoured for them to be able to love, could only comfort their misshapen fingers by stretching them out to the heat of the log fire which Cinderella built and lit in the vast echoing bedroom they shared, and had to keep going through the long cold winters.

Her name was really Ella. Cinder was a nickname – or a symbol: of what one cannot be sure. She was the burnt one perhaps. Or warmed by work and expectation. Frustration, disappointment – these came to her, but never iced her in.

So after the funeral her sisters' shoes got cleaned, the trays of leftovers were carried up the stone stairs and her sisters' log fire was coaxed into more sparkling, spitting, life and filled the inhospitable bedroom with a scent of pine which lulled its occupants to sleep, and nightmares of deprivation. The mulled wine briefly revived in the restless widower an optimism, a belief that all was not lost or need not be.

In this way, winter held.

But now it was Maytime. There was the scent of orange blossom to replace the sharper smell of pine log fires. Where there had been draughts were warm currents of air that caressed the cheeks and hands. The sun lit the darker corners of the kitchen. The copper pans took on their early summer life; and it was a special summer. As the sun approached its meridian the baron received a command to attend the royal celebration of the young prince-of-the-kingdom's coming of age. The prince was eighteen, seen to be handsome, reputed to be ardent, and known to be looking for a bride among the daughters of the peers of the realm. "He's sown his wild oats," people were saying, "and now wants to settle down." The invitation to the ball also requested the pleasure of the company of the baron's family.

It was years since he had had the privilege of being asked to present himself to the king and queen and he had feared being left out, which would have been the final blow to his self-esteem. A glass or two of wine now helped him to achieve that state of euphoria we call a sense of living now but paying later. He borrowed money. He bought a suit of the finest black velvet, the best black satin breeches and silk stockings money could buy, and – although he doubted he could dance and stay on his feet – dancing shoes with silver buckles. A snow-white shirt tricked out with exquisite lace cuffs and ruff completed the ensemble and showed that he was still half in mourning. As a precaution against stumbling on the palace steps as a result of too much wine before, during and after the gala night, he ordered to be made a stout ebony staff with a silver handle to which was to be tied a white satin bow.

He then bespoke the handsomest coach-for-hire from the public hiring stables – a magnificent and expensive equipage japanned in a black enamel so deep and rich you could see your reflection in it. He asked that upon its two doors there should be painted in silver-leaf a baron's coronet. To draw the coach he chose the best available pair of horses, one black, one white. He also bespoke the services of the sturdiest driver and the most comely footman and sent them to the tailor to be fitted out in livery of black and silver thread.

When the bills arrived he realised that all the money he had borrowed on the expectation that one of his three daughters would catch the prince's eye had gone, and more, yet still attracted interest as well as repayment. Now it was a question of how to fit his family out in a manner that would not diminish his own splendour.

He could not, himself, look into his dead wife's clothes press so asked Cinderella to do so because his two elder daughters were fully occupied by the daily visits of the most famous and expensive of the clever young men in the kingdom who helped women to look their best on grand occasions by smoothing wrinkles and experimenting with rose petal oils to soften the skin, and with powdered carnations that might simulate a blush. Of their services, the baron knew, his youngest daughter had no need.

"These will do beautifully, I think," Cinderella said, showing him the two dresses that remained in her mother's press, which she had looked after tenderly and hidden from bailiffs because they had been her mother's favourites. One of them was studded with rare black pearls and the other with rare white ones.

"Will they fit?" the baron asked, hardly trusting himself to look because of the memories they aroused. "And isn't there a third, for you?"

"They'll fit my sisters," she answered quietly, "so long as I let out a few seams and adjust the hems." Then she added, even more quietly, "Apart from my christening shawl, these are all there are," and waited hopefully for him to tell her in his mulled-wine expansive manner to call in the dressmaker to run up something for herself. He took a gulp of wine, then stared into the fire, then covered his eyes and said no more.

"Good night, papa," she whispered, and went upstairs for needle, scissors and thread.

Even to within an hour of the departure for the ball while she was tying her sisters' stays to try to accommodate their thickening waists to the dresses whose seams would not let out another fraction of an inch, running from one to the other, summoned by each in a cross-sounding but tremulous voice to ease this shoe on, stretch that garter, dab away the perspiration of hope or hopelessness from an enamelled cheek or a powdered shoulder, and then – alerted by the sound of splintering glass – dashing to her father's room to replace the clumsily dropped decanter, tie his ruff and the bow on his ebony cane, she was hoping for some magic wand to be waved that might transform her and take her to the ball too. When there was a loud knock on the castle door she ran down to open it, expectant of what she did not quite know. It was the comely footman, glittering in his livery of black and silver thread. "Tell your master and mistress the coach is here, love, will you?" he said, mistaking her for a servant.

"They are ready," she replied. "Wait. The baron is a little lame and may need help." She shut the door and called upstairs; and they came down, puffing and complaining and unsteadily, and tried not to catch her eye. But just before she reopened the door her sisters quietened and drew themselves up regally in a way which when the footman saw them made him stand to attention and bow his head, which made Cinderella glad for them because they had gone to a lot of trouble and put her to a lot of trouble to look their best.

She watched them go down the steps and enter the shining black coach that was to be drawn by the white horse and the black horse, then she shut the door, and paused, because there upon the floor of the immense hallway, barren of furniture, were one white pearl and one black pearl, fallen from her sisters' dresses. She picked them up. "They are my two horses," she murmured, "and my necklace. But where are my coach and gown?"

In her whole life she had never drunk anything but milk or water but now, having found a little mulled claret in her father's bedroom, taken it down to the kitchen and poured it into a mug, she sipped it and studied her reflection in the glass. Around her neck was the thread on which she had strung the two pearls, and around her shoulders her christening shawl. A thought came to her but she could not easily formulate it so she sat down by the chimney-piece thinking, "Well, here is my coach," poked the fire and waited for the white mice, her good companions, to come out of their hole, which they always did when she was alone. But tonight they were late.

She threw down some scraps of cheese (cards of invitation) and hummed some music to entice them. She picked a log from the bucket, put it on the fire to make a glow, a flame both of

memory and desire and of longing and of a tale and of the likeness
of tranquillity.

She took off her shoes and her patched stockings, put her
bare feet closer to the fire; and then (shyly as if uncertain of the
time of day) the mice emerged one by one. The flame of the
fire coloured the whiteness of their fur, enriched her shabby
dress. The mice nibbled at the cheese but then seemed to lose
interest in it as though nourished otherwise; clustered around
her feet, leapt, tumbled, to the sound of the music in her head,
rubbed softly against the chapped skin of her toes and ankles,
so that her feet felt encased in a pair of transparent crystal shoes
in which she believed she could dance not just through the night
but for ever.

And then the log suddenly emitted sparks that lit one by one
hundreds of chandeliers in the blackened stone of the chimney.
She shut her eyes and smiled. She touched the two pearls. They
seemed to her like a necklace and a crown. She felt for the ends
of the shawl but could not find them because the shawl had
become a gown in which transformed, transported, she could
dance through the as yet unlit corridors of the castle of her
history and her future in the arms of a man who would one day
love her and whom she would love.

When she opened her eyes the fire had all but gone out. The
clock that never chimed showed midnight. She lit fresh candles
from the one that was guttering and placed them in the hall as
a welcome home for her father and sisters, set some cold meats
and milk out for them, put the great oak door on the latch, lit
her own candle and climbed the tower; at every twist and turn
greeting or taking leave of her own shadow.

In her room she undressed, blew the candle out. She opened
the broken-paned ivy-clad window to the summer moonlight and
gazed out, resting her elbows on the sill, and realised that very
soon she would be sixteen and a grown woman and that although
as you left childhood behind you, you might have to go to a
funeral you did not have to go to a ball, because the ball would
come to you if you heard the music and saw the pictures in the
fire – and felt the presence, the touch of fingertips on your

cheeks, the touch of arms around your shoulders, of someone far away who wished you well.

She could hear the sound of merriment in the palace, so left her window open, got to bed, composed herself to sleep. There would be a lot to do tomorrow.

IRIS MURDOCH

IRIS MURDOCH

Iris Murdoch won the Booker Prize in 1978 with *The Sea, The Sea*. She has been shortlisted for the Prize more times – six – than any other author. She was born in Dublin of Anglo-Irish parents, spent her schooldays in London and Bristol and received her university education at Oxford and, later, at Cambridge. Since 1948 she has been a fellow of St Anne's College, Oxford, where for many years she taught philosophy. She still lives in Oxford with her husband, John Bayley. Iris Murdoch's first novel, *Under The Net*, was published in 1954. Among the honours and awards she has received since then are the CBE, the DBE, the James Tait Black Memorial Prize, the Whitbread Literary Award, the Booker Prize, and the Hamburg Shakespeare Prize.

AGAMEMNON CLASS 1939

In Memoriam Frank Thompson 1920–1944

Do you remember Professor
Eduard Fraenkel's endless
Class on the Agamemnon?
Between line eighty-three and line a thousand
It seemed to us our innocence
Was lost, our youth laid waste,
In that pellucid unforgiving air,
The aftermath experienced before,
Focused by dread into a lurid flicker,
A most uncanny composite of sun and rain.
Did we expect the war? What did we fear?
First love's incinerating crippling flame,
Or that it would appear
In public that we could not name
The aorist of some familiar verb.
The spirit's failure we knew nothing of,
Nothing really of sin or of pain,
The work of the knife and the axe,
How absolute death is,
Betrayal of lover and friend,
Of egotism the veiled crux,
Mistaking still for guilt
The anxiety of a child.
With exquisite dressage
We ruled a chaste soul.
They had not yet made an end
Of the returning hero.
The demons that travelled with us
Were still smiling in their sleep.

Heralded by the cries of hitherto silent Cassandra,
The undulating siren creates in the entrails
And in the heart new structures
Of sensation, the abrupt start
Of war, its smell and sound.
The hours distend with bombs,
The big guns vibrate in the ground.
Frightened men kill by remote control,
Or face to face, appalled, see their enemy fall.
Houses and public buildings with a kind of surprise
Bend their knees and turn into tombs.
Ever so many gentle worlds quietly end.
People sleep in catacombs.
White paths of doomed men
Daily criss-cross in the skies.
The sanctuary is bombed and lies
Open and unmysterious,
A garden of wild flowers.
Something crawls wounded on,
But the Holy One
Having suffered too long
Eventually dies.

Delphi medises and Apollo's face grows dim.
Was there a god there? We never saw him.
A priest was making a political sound.
Fey Helen lost her beauty and her shame,
Went home quite pertly in the end they say,
Piously helped the poor, became
A legend haunting a fought-over ground.
What was it for? Guides tell a garbled tale.
The hero's tomb is a disputed mound.
What really happened on that windy plain?
The young are bored by stories of the war.
And you the other young who stayed there
In the land of the past, are courteous and pale,
Aloof, holding your fates.
We have to tell you it was not in vain.

Even grief dates, and even Niobe
At last was fed, and you
Are all pain and yet without pain
As is the way of the dead.

No one can rebuild that town
And the soldier who came home
Has entered the machine of a continued doom.
Only the sky and the sea
Are unpolluted and old
And godless with innocence,
And twilight comes to the chasm
And to the sea's expanse
And the terrible bright Greek air fades away.

TOO LATE

What has she got left for her old admirer,
After a lifetime wed to the usurper?
When he was young he dreamed of being solitary;
The real aloneness later was another matter.
He needed then the thought of how she cried
At their brief meetings, and he carefully
Wrote the veiled letters which she not forbade,
Where high hopes hinted at were not denied.
His bright hair faded to a parching grey
And started to fall out. She never strayed;
Some cruder matters were not spoken of
In the long conversation of their love
Even their doubt was of obscure intent.
Death was not quick to take the thug away,
That death upon which they were both so bent
In a laconic upright sort of way.
(He thought, she's too discreet even to pray!)

Did he observe her sadness with some glee,
Savour the sense of her wild discontent,
Doleful and damned inside the situation?
Did guessing at her grief bring consolation
During his studied patience? Naturally he
Felt at her ruined life some satisfaction,
Could not be reasonably refused a gloat
About that ancient and disastrous error
Which she repented of over and over,
Her failure to choose this instead of that,
Which should have been dead easy! Yes, indeed,
Gloats he and checks, achieves no resignation.
Hard to remember now the early grace
Of love's unselfish rapturous elation.
Years passed in which he saw her lovely face
Lose all its quick response, grow desperate,
Thickened and slow, a sort of blinded look.
Grief is a secret worm, and even he,
He felt it crossly, was shut out.
Better perhaps. She would not later brook
What he might then have witnessed: better not to see.
Quite slowly she has made her terms with fate.
Her early charms disintegrate and sag.
She drinks a lot and has put on weight.
Objectively, she has become an old bag.
"Of course you're older, dear, but beautiful,
At least to me," he tells a tearful smile.
Life is a matter of choosing, ergo of losing,
They formulate when feeling philosophical.
Thank God at least no bloody kids arrived,
Doubtless because. He keeps a tactful style,
A sort of grim ironical gentleness
Being the atmosphere in which they have survived.
Letters, occasional meetings near her home
In office hours, as if by accident,
No travelling, an always urban scene,
And public, as if that meant innocent.
He has died in those tea shops, later in bars.

(They have lived through quite a lot of social change.)
Oh God, he was so young when it began, how strange, how
strange,
How worst of all that his own schemes
Were what destroyed his youth and his good looks
And his light heart and high IQ
And all those splendid dreams!
He might have written books, if she
Had been his wife, he would have made his mark;
Or if he'd had the sense to chuck her at the start,
And look for someone else, or just be free.
But vile emotions blocked his larger view
And early bafflement quite needlessly destroyed his life.
He turned to making money, even that
With only moderate success. His little flat
(To which she never came) is mean,
Provisional, just like a student's den.
Planning some final transformation scene,
He never bothered to try out his taste.
His hi-fi is unplayed, his books are chaste.
When all is makeshift art cannot bring peace.
At later times they talked about the south
And how they'd run away perhaps to Greece,
A place where tender veins of pebbles shine
In the still sea through deep transparent water.
At least in Maytime in an English field
To lie in buttercups he once besought her,
(The old swine being established as elsewhere
Fishing or something. Christ, he didn't care!)
To get away right out of London just for once
By car for half a day. She havered.
He ground his teeth and never quite forgave her.
Now he is testy, she apologizes.
Sometimes she would be sulky did she dare.
Their tragic story holds no more surprises.
He plays at leaving but can go nowhere.
At the longed-for last he has gained a ghost.
She timidly proposes this and that.

Can they start life anew? What life and how?
He stays on in his flat and wants no changes now.
Does he desire her? No. The welcome death
Emancipates, it seems, not her but him.
Even at this late hour he'll have some fun.
Now that his sacrifice is over and proved vain
He won't be fooled again, he's not yet done.
What is she crying for – her vanished youth?
I too was beautiful when I was young.
Or is she crying for that bloody man,
For her dead husband, for the real one?

MUSIC IN IRELAND

While we are hearing Mozart in this barn
Rain clatters on the roof
Which is made of corrugated iron
Or some such stuff.
Mozart can manage all the same
To elevate the noisy rain
Into a delicate suspended dome
Or ceremonial tent with glittering fringes,
Making it very taut and still.
The barn is rather damp and chill
And people's clothes give off a cold steam
A somewhat awkward wet and woollen smell.
Afterwards there will be tea and scones
And dark blackcurrant jam
And a guided tour of the house.

We are in Ireland.
Murders are planned in time at certain hours
In homely kitchens when the meal is finished
By thoughtful men sitting beside turf fires

Over a drink with comradeship and wit
Especially at weekends when leisure comes
For planting bombs, the weekly labour done.
Monday will bring again
The breaking of the news to families,
The life sentence of the child witness,
The maimed beloved in the wheel chair,
The condemnation to unending pain, and tears
Which have nothing to do with Mozart.

Near by on Strangford Lough
Migrating geese bound for the Arctic Zone,
Stand solemnly upon the glossy mud
In the brown twilight of the afternoon,
Soon to move on toward the midnight sun
With empty hills of snow to walk upon,
But now are waiting, dignified and sad,
Big heavy birds obedient to God,
Closely observed by the local bird-watching society
Against a misty background of factory chimneys.

Murder is abstract, something not imagined
In detail or defined as such,
Negating love and mercy, hideous
Schema of a hating mind.
This music too is a material
That's not entirely human,
Instant and imageless as angels are,
Absolute in formation as the snow crystal,
Of necessity the aloof laughter,
Of undeserved delight the avatar,
Hinting the rhythm of the planet.

This is the matrix that we cannot fathom,
It is our response that is human,
Our restless yearning in the day's event
Our temporal desire for resolution,
Our confused sense of a before and after.

The music lifts like steam
The secret cares of hearers
Tired with cold and rain
And intermittent dream
Of their own sorrows and the old
Sorrows of Ireland,
Which they try to banish.
Heads bowed down or thrown
Backward open-eyed
Here and there are dark
With terrible deaf pictures.
Sounds rise up and vanish
Into a pitted dome.
It continues to rain.
The acoustics being imperfect some people fidget.

Something which is pure has come
To a high magnetic field.
Cry out as it passes on,
When shall we be healed?

JOHN SEES A STORK AT ZAMORA

Walking among quiet people out from mass
He saw a sudden stork `
Fly from its nest upon a house.
So blue the sky, the bird so white,
For all these people an accustomed sight.

He took his hat off in sheer surprise
And stood and threw his arms out wide
Letting the people pass
Him by on either side
Aware of nothing but the stork-arise.

On a black tapestry now
This gesture of joy
So absolutely you.

PENELOPE FITZGERALD

PENELOPE FITZGERALD

Penelope Fitzgerald, like her mother and grandmother, was educated at Somerville College, Oxford. She has worked in journalism, the Ministry of Food, a bookshop and various schools. She even once ran an all-night coffee stall. While she has written biographies of Burne-Jones, the Knox brothers and Charlotte Mew, her first novel, *The Bookshop*, was shortlisted for the Booker in 1978 as was her most recent novel, *The Beginning of Spring* in 1988; and she won with *Offshore* in 1979. The book was based on her experiences of living on a Thames barge moored at Chelsea Harbour. It eventually sank.

The Likeness

Make no mistake, you pay for every drop of blood in your body.

Demetrius Christiaki was anxious, as far as possible, to please his father, who was a cotton importer, and still wore on his watch-chain one of the gold 100 lira pieces which had been brought away out of Stamboul fifty years before when the family escaped to London. Father and son had had a number of disagreements, but not, fortunately, about Dimi's choice of career. He trained as an artist, in London with Luke Fildes, and in Paris with Gérôme. The Christiaki were prosperous but they were not materialists. In 1880, when Dimi was twenty, his father asked him to go to Stamboul to paint a portrait of his aunt.

Aunt Calliope (in reality the cousin of a great aunt) belonged to a branch of the family which had chosen to stay behind in Turkey after the troubles. She lived alone, except for her servants and a great niece, in the Greek district, the Fener. She must be over seventy by this time, and was said to be in poor health. Dimi's father had a splendid collection of family portraits by Watts which he intended to leave to the South Kensington Museum, on condition that it should always be on show to the public, free of charge. It was almost complete, all the older generation were there save one only Calliope was missing.

"I don't see why Watts refuses to go," said Dimi. "I believe he's in Venice."

"He hasn't refused, I haven't asked him. His digestion has become very weak, it would be madness for him to attempt the crossing."

"He gets a very good likeness."

"I have had you trained for three years," said his father. "Are you afraid?"

"Yes," said Dimi.

Christiaki senior ignored this, and went on: "Good, well, I shall say nothing in my letter about either your drawing or your painting, you will explain my wishes in person. Go gently, remember you will be in the Fener, not in Alexandria."

"My aunt may not want me to paint her portrait."

"It will be your business to persuade her that you are competent."

"I meant that she might not welcome the whole idea."

"In any case, she will welcome a relative."

Dimi had not been to Stamboul since he was ten, a schoolboy on holiday. Some things about it he could remember vividly, others not at all. The sober hush of the Fener, terribly depressing to a ten-year-old, came back to him, and the relief of being taken out sailing almost as far as the mouth of the Black Sea. He recalled very clearly that in his aunt's house there was a well, or spring, which had been blessed four hundred years ago by St Akakios the Harmless. At the time Dimi had drunk the water with reverence, confident that it would help him to pass his school tests.

He travelled by *Messageries Maritimes* via Marseilles and arrived just before nightfall, when the city which will last as long as there are men on earth looked at its most enticing, not bettered by any engraving, its outline just at the point of disappearing into a pearl-grey sky. The Karaköy wharf, on the other hand, and even the Yeni mosque nearby, proved as they drew near to be black with smoke from the coal-burning ferries, while the water was crowded beyond belief with longshore traffic. Against the wooden piers of the Galata Bridge, filth and rubbish rode high. Shoals of fish, which had swarmed across to feed on human refuse, were hooked, gutted, fried and offered for sale in the cook-boats, consumers consumed.

Perhaps, Dimi thought, he ought to have travelled more respectably. But he was hardly established yet as a portrait painter, and it was a rule of the Christiaki that what you have not earned on your own account you must not spend. If, when they were children, they were tipped sixpence or a shilling by some visiting man of business, they were required to give it back at once, with the explanation "I have done nothing that you should give me this." And if the kindly guest had turned away and was no longer listening, one had to tug at his sleeve and repeat the words louder. Surely no duty in later life could be more embarrassing than that. Dimi let his thoughts wander a little. He would arrive late, but he knew that there are moments when to keep count of time is to waste it. Half way up the Golden Horn the ferryboat's engines faltered, and it had grown quite dark by the time they drifted, apparently at random, against the walls of the Fener Iskalesi. High above him, and above the sea walls of the city, he could see the discreet lights of the Fener.

Dimi's feet knew these streets. As he walked through the Petri, carrying his one carpet bag, the high cloud drifted apart and showed him that the pavement widened a little to form a kind of square where two domed churches, sunken with age, faced one another. There was one light burning in the barred window of the night baker, who was preparing the church bread. Dimi turned a corner and went down three steps set at an angle to a blank doorway, deep in its stone recess.

Ten years ago a black woman who stood no nonsense had been on duty at the door. When he heard her voice at the grating he remembered her name, and said: "Ferahidil, it's Demetrius, Demetrius from England."

"Where is your servant?"

"I don't travel with a servant," he said. "I'm an artist."

One after another she drew back the bolts. As he crossed the forecourt behind her he could just see the reflections of her lamp in the gold of the icons, and make out the position of the holy well. Ferahidil let him come only as far as the ante-room. Then she lit another lamp and left him alone while she fetched the coffee. This at least meant that he could consider himself received as a guest.

A young girl, however, came back with the silver tray, the two glasses of water, the two spoonfuls of jam. She was in

Turkish dress, as though this – it was two o'clock in the morning – was a party, with bare feet in red leather *tsarouchia*. To the exhausted Dimi her prettiness seemed an injustice. He knew it must be Cousin Evgenia. She must have been about five, as plain as a frog, and he had taught her, with the help of a few sweets from the bazaar, to count in English.

"Why aren't you in bed and asleep?" he asked.

"Tantine is in bed, I am staying up for you. Why didn't you come earlier? We sent a *hamal* down to Karaköy for your luggage, he has been there for two days."

"I haven't any luggage," Dimi said. "I hope he won't wait there much longer." First sitting upright on a chair, but then giving it up for a cushion, she chattered on in Greek, Turkish, French and English without much distinction between them. She couldn't, however, quite get the English "j", so that she spoke of jam as *zham*, and journey as *zhourney*. This was a relief to Dimi and enabled him, for the first time since he arrived, not to feel at a disadvantage.

Early on the following morning he was called down to the salon to pay his respects to his aunt. This room again he half remembered. It was in the Turkish style, with six pairs of windows shedding their latticed cross lights on to the seats of honour at the far end. But the furniture was French, and sight was obstructed by an immense grand piano made in Berlin and loaded down with Bohemian glass, piles of old journals and a bronze head of Gladstone by Alphonse Legros. Aunt Calliope, much smaller and thinner than he had expected, held out her hand to him from the "angle" beneath the right-hand window.

"Welcome, you have come."

"Welcome, I have found you," Dimi replied automatically, scarcely feeling that he spoke the truth, she looked so much worn away. She began to talk about his father, adding mildly: "Well, we are quite out of the world here, you have come from England to set us right."

"Why should you think that I want to do that?" Dimi cried in distress. "Do you think my father sent me over here to insult you?"

His aunt smiled. "You are shouting. What would your English friends say?"

Dimi paused. "They would say 'Steady on, old fellow.'"

"Steady on, old fellow," she repeated in English, doubtfully.

With some idea of showing the worth or seriousness of his training he began to talk about the bust of Gladstone. He had met Legros often enough and could say that he knew him quite well.

"He lives in London, but he is French?" Aunt Calliope asked.

"Burgundian."

"Is it true that he can't read or write?"

"It may be true," said Dimi, "but there's no way of telling." He felt that he was losing her attention because he hadn't begun by saying something about the spiritual value of art. Everything in the room must have a higher importance for her, even the rubbish on top of the piano. Evidently she tired very easily. She told him that she regretted she would have to rest a good deal of the day, because old friends would be coming in that evening for the express purpose of meeting him.

"Meanwhile, my dear, you have all you want, you are at home?"

Dimi considered. "Perhaps I'm not quite at ease yet. Last night, when I arrived, I was angry with myself because I thought my cousin ought still to be five years old."

"You don't want change?"

"I want progress, Tantine, certainly I do."

"Well," she said, "my Evgenia is still at school."

While his aunt had been speaking Dimi had begun the study of her face from a professional point of view, calculating, as he had been taught, the primary, secondary and reflected lights. Her age could be indicated, he thought, without heavy shadows, simply by care with the flesh tones. But for some reason he did not like to suggest a preliminary sitting, not now, not yet. He might start by doing a few sketches from memory in his room, which overlooked the sea.

Ferahidil, with an attendant maid, came to take her mistress up to rest. At midday Evgenia returned, no longer, thank heavens, in fancy dress but in the uniform of her *gymnase*, with plain gold studs in her ears. The two of them sat down together at the low dining table, so that Dimi, who had been uneasily conscious of the heaps of scarcely-worn red slippers in the corners of the room, waiting to be given to the poor, and each one lightly marked by her foot's impress, now found himself near enough to watch her breathing. The uniform confused him.

"Who are these people who are coming this evening?" he asked her. "Of course you must know them all."

"I know them." He thought she was going to go through the names, but she only said "I hate them."

Dimi felt he couldn't let this pass, even if it was said for effect. "What have they done to offend you? Anyway, they will be guests in Tantine's house, and it's out of the question . . ."

It was not a success. At home he himself was the wild one, the Bohemian. He had practice in ignoring reproofs, none in giving them. Evgenia gave him a bright glance.

"Steady on, old fellow."

"Where did you learn that?"

"I don't know. When I came back they were all saying it in the kitchen."

Since it was a fast day they were served with fish and a cheese dish. The flaky pastry was so light that it was difficult to manage; not, however, for Evgenia, who held her fork in her left hand, but ate *alla turca* with two fingers and her right thumb. It was dexterous, but not quite civilised. He wished very much that he could make a drawing of her. That, however, would make her conceited, and it was not what he had come to Stamboul to do. Presently she threw down her fork and said: "Well, now you've come at last you can take me out into the city."

"Haven't you got afternoon classes?"

"Not now, not till later."

"But where do you want to go?"

"Anywhere. You can take me to church."

"Which church?"

"To St Theodosia. There's a service of blessing there this afternoon for Professor Zographos."

"But I've no idea who he is."

"He died three years ago. When they last looked at the corpse it was not corrupted. The family are afraid that he is possessed by some other spirit."

"Professor Zographos was a teacher?"

"Yes, at the college."

"What did he teach?"

"Anatomy," said Evgenia absently.

"And what will they do if he holds up for another three years?"

"What would anyone do, cousin? Boil his bones clean."

She began to eat again and he turned the conversation to her studies. There was a new subject in the final year, psychology, but it did not interest her. Drawing, painting? No, she did none at all. But music she loved. Her piano was the only one in the Fener, probably therefore the only one in Stamboul. When it was time for her to go to London, Dimi must take her to concerts, she had never heard an orchestra play. Dimi replied that he would be happy to take her to a Wagner concert and to present her to Mme Wagner, whom he knew slightly. "Oh, cousin, yes, I beseech you . . ." She had turned pink, a pale rose colour, delightful. So far, so good. No more on the subject of Professor Zographos.

But at that moment, something having been muttered by a servant as the glutinous desserts, powdered with fine sugar, were handed round, Evgenia declared that they ought to go out at once. Ferahidil wanted to fumigate the rooms on the ground floor. There was a hostile presence in the house. The servant, referring to it, had made the familiar sign to avert the evil eye. Ferahidil was never mistaken, it seemed.

"And what does she do?"

"She used to burn sage plant, to drive out the evil."

"And now?"

"Now we give her something modern, something from the English warehouse, Zheyes Fluid."

And this is my cousin, Dimi said aloud to the sea, the sky and the clouds, or rather this is my great aunt's cousin's great niece. Corpses possessed, the houses exorcised with Jeyes Fluid. This is the Fener, I am a Greek, I am among Greeks, and yet I might as well be in Tibet.

He left Evgenia by herself to drink her coffee and crossed over on the next ferry to the Pera. At the end of the week his friends from London should be arriving – Haynes Williams, Philip Cassell and his sister Fanny, and Haynes' new wife who was rather older than Haynes and would act, presumably, as a chaperone to the whole party. All four of them were artists, all of them intended to sketch picturesque oriental subjects. "We must meet your aunt," they had said, "we must meet this young cousin of yours. If you asked her, she might like to model for us."

"She mustn't feel afraid of us!" said Mrs Haynes in a faint shriek.

Haynes wanted to have a go at the graveyard of Karaca Ahmet by moonlight. It would be a selling subject, he thought, for a steel engraving. Mrs Haynes dressed rather smartly, which must cost him a good deal.

They had booked rooms in the Hotel Jockey, in a street just off the Grand' Rue. They would have preferred the Fener, so as to be as near to Dimi as possible, but in the Fener there were no hotels. All who came there were Greeks, and every Greek could find a relation of some kind, however distant, to stay with. The Hotel Jockey, unfortunately, was quite without character. Dimi checked the price per night and per week. He told himself that he was looking forward to the arrival of his friends.

That evening the house still smelled a little of disinfectant, but it was splendidly lit, almost like his father's house in Holland Park. Evgenia took up her correct place in the ante-room, ready to help receive the guests. She was in white, which suited her less well than her Turkish outfit. She looked older, and wore European shoes.

As dusk fell a few elderly men – but each of them accompanied by more than one elderly lady, so that the salon soon filled – came in from the houses round about. Everyone talked about what had occupied them during the day, before the great city sank into the twilight of unsatisfied desires. The men, who had their little mannerisms, talked about profit and loss. The ladies surrounded Dimi, gently reminding him, or more often telling him for the first time, of family relationships. Only one guest circulated between the sexes. Perhaps, indeed, that was his function. He was apparently an indispensable man, prepared to laugh or be laughed at, just as the fish beneath the Galata Bridge were ready to eat or be eaten.

There were too many women at the soirée. It was interesting, however, to talk to old Mme Sevastopolo, a relic, a skeleton, thinner even than Tantine, who when she had last been in London, as a child, had seen Byron's coffin passing through the streets. "The doctors killed the great poet," said Dimi. "That wouldn't happen now."

Mme Sevastopolo looked at him in surprise. "Why not?"

While they stood talking Babikian began to flit from dish to dish, sampling a little of everything.

"He looks as though he had known what starvation is," said Dimi.

"Oh, I think you aren't right," Mme Sevastopolo replied. "In my experience those who have starved are never greedy," and then, looking round the salon, "But where is Evgenia?"

"She left us quite a few minutes ago," said Babikian. "But Mr Christiaki will be able to tell us exactly." Taking Dimi by the elbow, softly urging and squeezing, he persuaded him into one of the many little alcoves along the opposite side of the room. "How well do you know your cousin?" he asked.

"Not well at all," said Dimi. "She was a child when I last saw her."

"A touch of eccentricity there. So pretty, but perhaps even a little mad. But what would you say is the most noticeable change in her, beyond the development of the breasts? They, of course, are remarkable. I am speaking to you as an artist."

Dimi trembled. "I don't know whether you think I find you amusing, Babikian."

"Oh, you must call me Baby, otherwise people may think you take me seriously."

The soirée did not last long. By eleven o'clock there was a stir among the faded guests, who wished before they left to say goodnight to Evgenia, although they all lived in the Fener and might expect to see her every day. Still she did not come, but Tantine made no apologies. The visitors' servants began to emerge from the kitchen to light their lanterns and dip their hands in the water of the holy well. Mme Sevastopolo embraced Dimi and asked him, when he got back to London, to visit the graves of her relatives. "They are all interred at Shooter's Hill. Perhaps you know this hill?"

As soon as the last group of them moved away, still talking, the men's voices higher than the women's, Babikian a kind of *alto continuo* to be heard above the rest, the bright lights were all lowered, not for reasons of economy, but to return the house to its usual state of half-mourning, the seclusion of the Fener.

The next day his aunt asked him whether it had crossed his mind that he might marry Evgenia.

WILLIAM GOLDING

WILLIAM GOLDING

William Golding was born in Cornwall in 1911 and educated at Marlborough College Grammar School and Brasenose College, Oxford. He published a volume of poems in 1935 and taught at Bishop Wandsworth's School, Salisbury. In 1940 he joined the Royal Navy where he spent the next five years, finishing as Lieutenant in command of a rocket ship. His first novel, *Lord of The Flies*, was published in 1954 and filmed by Peter Brook in 1963. *Rites of Passage* won the Booker Prize in 1980. He was awarded the Nobel Prize in 1983 and knighted in 1988.

Caveat Emptor

Conan raised his eyebrows in stage astonishment. "You? Writing for charity?"

"You don't believe in my finer feelings? Well you are quite right. They twisted my arm."

He nodded. "When I think of the old days—"

"So I have to find a short story. *Have* to!"

"Stay the night, Wilfred. You'll think of something."

He let me find my own way up the narrow stairs. I knew the cottage as well as he did, the uneven floors, the low beams, the thatched eaves in their chicken wire. By the time I had been to the loo and put out my few things I could hear him arguing with someone. I went downstairs in time to hear the tradesman's parting shot. "Then you can take your custom elsewhere, Mr Duffy, and you'll be hearing from me."

"No sense of service," said Conan to the man's back. "Helen never liked him."

"I was sorry to hear about her accident."

"Well you always wanted her more than I did."

"Oh I say!"

His instinct told him it was the right moment. "Spare me a tenner."

I gave it him ruefully. At the best of times he was the sort of brazen man it is impossible to refuse unless you are of the same sort. "You were never afraid to ask, were you?"

"You might make it two tens. No. Three. Thanks. English diffidence! I think you're all proud of it. Diffidence and the Protestant work ethic."

Their sitting room hadn't changed much, just grown a bit shabbier the way houses do if there are no permanent women

about. There were still horsey pictures on the walls, a photograph of Helen on horseback and some of her own daubs. As
she had been, they were precise and – yes – dull. "You didn't
both ride?"

"No. Just Helen, regular as clockwork, Mondays and Thurs-
days. Nothing beyond a canter. No jumping, just hacking. I think
she really liked the dressing up."

"So you weren't with her when–"

"No. I wasn't with her *when*. If you'd care to amuse yourself
there's a few inches of whisky left in the bottle – I'll just nip
down to the butcher's with these."

"These" were the three ten pound notes. He considered them
for a while. He glanced at the photograph of Helen then back at
me. He made his instant decision. "No butcher. Those were
twenties I saw in your wallet. You really do need a story?"

"Oh for God's sake – when do I not? You think they grow like
blackberries?"

"Add a twenty to these three and I'll give you your story."

"You're not a writer!"

"A genuine twenty-four carat extraordinary story for fifty
quid."

"That's a lot of money even today. Remember I'm doing it
for charity."

"I'm not. *And* a meal this evening at the pub. The food's
reasonable."

I attempted to bargain but the result was inevitable. He
snapped the note then put it away with the others in some
pocket or other. He went away for a few moments and came
back with a three-quarter-full bottle of red wine. I looked at the
label. "You do yourself well."

"Tick. Hand to mouth."

"Didn't Helen–?"

"Took it with her."

"That's a well-known impossibility."

He was silent for a while, pouring from the bottle. Then –
"Kept man. Way back in the twenties my father used to say, 'If
there's one thing worse than a kept woman it's a kept man –
bedad!'"

"He never said 'bedad!'"

"Probably not."

"This story–"

"Scene – the south of France. The south-west in fact. Foot-hills, snow, lakes, mountain roads, that sort of thing. English couple honeymooning after the war. Remember the mess Europe was in? Black market, resistance feuds, loot – the whole mess in fact."

"Europe for our generation."

"The mess was still there when we went honeymooning, Helen and I – all under the surface. It's still there, smouldering like a banked up bonfire. Then there would be a flare-up. Someone done in."

"If you say so. Personally–"

"Our honeymoon in all that. Did you know? She was a virgin! Disgusting. Blood and snot."

"She was beautiful."

"If you like a statue. Come on Wilfred! You knew all the time it was for her money! I cringed for that – said to myself I'd stand up straight later. No, I'm not ashamed – 'bedad', so to speak. People with money are admirable. Why not? They don't have to contrive, can afford honesty, don't have to lie so much."

"She wasn't rich."

"Helen? Good God, no. I mean–" He spoke with sudden passion "– I adore the rich! That rudeness! It's a kind of strength. Helen had no more than what you'd call a sort of competence. Don't you remember how good-looking I was?"

"When does the story start? Come on! Events! Be insightful! Extend our perceptions of contemporary reality! A bit more *blague*, old friend."

"All right. There's no reason why I should not Tell All. No evidence one way or the other. It was that damned virginity. I'd hurt her you see. She was – don't the Germans call that kind of girl a 'shield maiden'? Anyway the day after, she went to bed in the afternoon and forbade me to follow. In fact she retired hurt."

He took a sip and thought for a while.

"Where was I? Yes. You know, my father, he told me, 'Son', he said–"

"Bedad."

"I concede the bedad. He said 'When dealing with a woman, begin the way you mean to go on.'"

"He wasn't very original, was he?"

"I'd planned to do just that and show her gently but firmly who was boss. I remarked that I'd go down to the bar for a bit. But she wouldn't have it. Took the boss's job off my hands."

"I care for that. Here's to Helen!"

"She sent me out. 'Leave the bar alone,' she said. 'You go and paint. You can take my things.' Imagine that, a woman hauling her painting gear along on a honeymoon!"

"No, no, no. I just don't believe. You'll have to do better than that!"

"'You go and paint me a picture,' she said, 'after what you've done!'"

"It's a professional point, Conan. Motivation! No one, but no one is going to believe she would do that or say that!"

"Patience. Good God, she stood me in the corner. I wonder what she had been expecting the night before? A flight into heaven?"

"I repeat, you're not convincing me."

"Anyway, I traipsed off into the foothills with a load of her kit and holed up just off the road by the lake and well hidden from any direction but across the water. I was feeling self-conscious, believe it or not."

"Impossibilities on top of implausibilities."

"That's your affair, Wilfred. I am giving you your fifty quid's worth – not forgetting tonight's dinner. I can still remember the gloom with which I sat before the easel and contemplated an unblemished rectangle of canvas, white as our marriage looked like being – so I stared at the canvas and in the end it hypnotised me rather nastily and a lot of war experiences came and performed on it. After that or during it I fell asleep with a brush dropped from my hand and my head more or less on my knees."

"That's better. I can go with that."

"What woke me up was the sound of a plane crashing and an

almighty blow on the head. In fact the blow was so excruciating
it nearly put me to sleep again. I picked myself up and fell down
again by the water and even as I was falling I realised it wasn't
a plane but a car or van going hell-for-leather and as I realised
that I heard another one coming. It was instinct which made me
keep my head down until the second car was past – you remember? All the hassle of the resistance, settling wartime scores –
a stray Irishman wouldn't have been more than a quick look and
a short burst from a laughing fellow rover."

"They didn't see you?"

"If they did, neither of them stopped to tell me. In a minute
or two the lake and the road were as silent as a television set
with the sound turned off. Just a lot of green hills and water not
moving. It was only then that I found what my face was resting
on. It was a rectangular paper parcel and I swear that I knew
all the complicated truth in that split second and only came up
with the improbabilities later. You see, this was life. Improbabilities are what happen. One car had been chasing the other.
Number one car had been getting rid of loot the quickest way –
probably meant it for the lake and clouted my head instead. I
took a quick look round, found the landscape was as deserted
as ever and unwrapped the parcel. Of course it was a picture.
What else? Loot! *I* don't know anything about pictures but you
wouldn't bother to throw last year's calendar out of a car while
being chased by other villains would you? So I turned it
right side up and my God it clouted me over the head all over
again."

"Go on!"

"You see the real thing – I know it from those few moments
– is *immediacy*. There it was, not in an art gallery or the window
of a shop or in some institute – it was stuff in my hands, colour
in my very private eye, a blinder, and I learnt more about art in
those seconds than I could have got from years among the
academics."

"I wonder if I can bring that off?"

"Look. The experience was powerful and subtle and wholly
unexpected. That picture spoke with the brutal authority of
something which had literally hit me over the head!"

"I'm not with you."

"I threw the paper in the lake and looked the thing over inch by inch. That sun – less a sun than a swirl of, of supernova! Everything was cosmic violence, a tree like a tornado, purple atmosphere, a world not so much turning as spinning. I tell you, Wilfred, it was *deafening*!"

"I can use that."

"There was the signature too. Vincent van Gogh."

"You could probably look it up."

He paused for a while. Then – "I swear these hands have sweatily held a prime example of – what? You know the irises fetched more than twenty million? Of course in those days this wouldn't have fetched half as much, but enough, oh my God yes, more than enough! I had it there in my hands, a fortune which would set me free to beat hell out of Helen before leaving. Also a fortune which the people in the second car would come looking for as soon as they discovered it was missing. What is more they would be playing for keeps."

"You never considered doing the honest thing? The reward might have been worth it."

"Be your age. Or rather be the age we were when all this–"

"Either happened or did not happen."

"Can you imagine me turning up at some gallery and saying 'This fell off the back of a truck. I want to know if it's worth anything.' I'd have finished up inside a prison. Have you ever been in a French prison?"

"Only visiting."

"What was I to do? Couldn't give it back! Couldn't throw it away – couldn't sell it in France. I didn't know the continental form well enough to dabble in *that* market. So I had to hide the canvas, then get it through customs into England."

"What about Helen? You couldn't hide it from her."

"Oh yes I could. In fact it was only then that I realised that God was trying to tell me something. He was being very, very good. He'd given me the perfect set-up for hiding a picture. I could make sure no one would even touch it since the paint would be fresh on and still tacky."

"You wouldn't – you didn't – dare!"

"It was mine wasn't it? Morally I mean. Oh of course I felt a qualm or two but mostly about the villains coming back and catching me before I'd done. Then too, I knew nothing about the business but was trusting that it could be cleaned of my disguise and restored when finally I wanted to dispose of it. I was starting from scratch. I was virgin in the matter as Helen had been in hers. Then again, all I knew about your actual painting operation was that you mixed your colours with Chinese white to taste – that's right isn't it?"

"Probably. I forget."

"I couldn't take it straight back to the hotel. Helen was too dull to be anything but honest. She'd turn it in and be satisfied with her picture in the papers. There was another thing too. Van Gogh wasn't cooperating. The bastard dumped his colours on the canvas by the bucketful. Here and there it came up in bloody great heaps–"

"*Impasto* they call it."

"Thanks. A blind man could have traced the shapes in that picture. He could even feel the stalks of whatever it was made such a blazing yellow crop. As for the mountains – but most of all the sun! He'd just squeezed a tube on to the canvas then brought it round in a swirl the way a pastry cook uses piping! It stood up. I hadn't been smearing on colour for more than a minute or two before I realised the size of the job in front of me. I stopped scrubbing and thought. One way would be to cover the canvas so deep there'd be a new, smooth surface. But with what? There wasn't enough stuff in Helen's box. I thought of using mud from the verge of the lake but saw that it would dry and flake off. I thought of a chef's icing too! I thought of some surprising substances one way and another but saw in the end that I couldn't obliterate the picture. All I could do was disguise it, the way a false nose and moustache might disguise a face. So imagine me working away with Helen's palette knife or the wrong end of her biggest brush or even my thumb – *anything*, in fact, but the hairs which were meant for the job! D'you know that I came to understand him? In a way I was even closer than mere immediacy, wasn't I? They say that black magic relies on violation. There's something in it, Wilfred. As you defile the works of man or God you come closer to the being of the maker than you can get in any other way. I was, you might say, taking his work apart. I was breaking it. I felt that picture, I even began to suffer with it, with him. He'd smeared a line with his thumb, a hedge, I guess it was though by then I wasn't bothered by what anything meant. That smear had come right up through him from the very soles of his feet!"

"Synaesthesia."

"What's that?"

"What you claim to have experienced."

"It's true I tell you! I'd been let into him, himself, his nature, saw things his way, morbid as it was, morbid and, what's the word – apocalyptic with a brilliant and tragic splendour."

"Bravo! That was a cadenza."

"Of course you don't understand."

"I supplied a word most people don't even know!"

"Oh the things I knew then about painting, about art, which I can't say, can't paint, can't even believe now as the years roll over me!"

He was silent.

"Conan. The story."

"Well. I gave Vincent four more of his sun-swirls but I told myself they were the heads of flowers. And so on. There was a more-or-less rectangular field. I made it the lopsided pot which held them. I exhausted Helen's paints, Chinese white and all. Then I fixed the thing face down in her box, prayed the colours wouldn't run, packed up and fled to the hotel."

"How big was the box?"

He thought, then smiled at me, wickedly.

"Just big enough to take the painting. When I got back Helen insisted on seeing it. Now what happened then is going to strain your credulity."

"You underestimate me."

"When she saw the picture she fell in love with me all over again. If it was love, that is. I wonder why I never throttled her? She said she'd never understood the full extent of my maleness, imagine that, me, a pensioner of hers. But how ridiculous! She swore I must continue to paint. Before I knew

where I was we were cutting our honeymoon short and that
suited me because in the evening when the French news came
on the radio with a hiss and crackle we heard that a car had been
found abandoned with two dead bodies, both car and bodies
riddled. That was less than ten miles from the lake! If I'd wanted
proof that the picture was genuine that was good enough. Helen
was surprised how eagerly I agreed we must leave for home. I
may say she gave me the nastiest five minutes of my life in
customs. She insisted on the man looking at my work and he
examined it so long he might have painted it himself. I couldn't
catch my breath. Then he said, *'Madame a raison. C'est extra,
ça.'* I had felt I was going a beetroot colour but if he noticed me
he must have thought it was pride. The English side was easy
of course. They just waved us through. I took a trivial precaution
by initialling the picture – proof of ownership! – and hung it in
the dark corner half-way up the stairs. Helen tried at once to
make an artist of me. I resisted. Oh I did some painting! Mostly
impasto – you see I'd worked out the first step towards getting
my hands on the million hidden under my blobs of paint. I needed
an accurate copy of my own work – including his – before I could
begin any negotiations."

"You've never become an artist on the one hand or appeared
in society as the owner of a million on the other."

"Helen accepted at last that some sort of miracle had happened
with my 'first picture'. You can't repeat miracles. Besides we
were both otherwise occupied some of the time. She was no
longer sore and demanded her rights. Rites. My God what rites
they were! She even began to forget the picture and then she
had her accident. I was in town at the time. They got hold of
me and I came rushing back. She'd been found on the downs
with her neck broken and her horse waiting stolidly on the other
side of the hedge. The coroner said we must accept riding as a
risk sport. Accidental death. Do you know it was only a day
or two after the inquest that I found that my picture – my
superimposed picture with the million pounds under it – had
been stolen! They took nothing else. After all there was nothing
even remotely near that class. They knew what they wanted.
But the coincidence! After I'd recovered from the shocks I

visited the place where she died. It was like the car chase. I mean the thing was obvious. She never jumped. The horse hadn't gone back to stables the way they do, because he was in a field with a gate that closed itself – clash!"

"No! No! No!"

"They must have smelled their way back up that French road yard by yard. Here and there were cottages. They must have enquired for a friend – they'd lost touch with him. Then the hotel – who was stopping there, when? In those days, Wilfred, you will remember that a French hotel register really meant something, not like now! A honeymoon couple, a Madame *et* Monsieur Duffy. Tell us about them please, they *sound* like our old friends! Money rustles. Monsieur will see that they left quickly though they were booked for longer. Yes, they had painting materials."

"This is paranoid!"

"What words you know. But they found us, didn't they? I talked to the farmer who had come across the body. He was communicative. He said her friends hadn't ridden past since the accident. Her friends."

"Look, Conan. The whole thing doesn't hang together. There are huge gaps, there are unmotivated actions. You've been watching–"

"–too much television. Yes."

"I'm sorry. But really!"

"My dear Wilfred, you bought it. I have your fifty pounds and this evening I'll add a free meal to them."

"I simply don't believe the story."

"If you need to that's your problem isn't it? As I said, I've given you a story. I didn't say I'd write it for you. Besides – what was it – gaps? Unmotivated actions? Implausibilities? Don't you see? That's life."

"Not like my life it isn't."

"Well there. You and your word processor! It's your job to sew the sides of the gaps together, motivate the actions, make the implausible plausible. As I said, you bought it; and as the boring old Romans said: Let the buyer beware!"

"So she never knew."

"It hung on our stairs for five years. A million. More. Two? Ten?"

"They couldn't sell it."

"What's that to me? It'll be somewhere in South America by now, or North America."

"Aren't you ever scared? After all, you were more concerned than she was."

"Not by their way of thinking."

"I've caught you, haven't I? You've made up the whole thing!"

"Like I told you I took precautions. I put very small initials in the bottom left hand corner."

"So?"

I thought that for a while he was unwilling to go on.

"Not my initials."

"Hers!"

I found I was standing up.

"Conan! They killed her!"

"Damn it man. What was I to do? Your character had to cover himself hadn't he? I had to cover myself hadn't I? I might have been sent down for years and maybe in a French gaol too! In any case I didn't know that the outcome would be – terminal. Do we have to go into that?"

"I don't know where I am. Who is what, where is which – is it true?"

"Is any story true? Write your story. Have it. No one will believe you for all the evidence is gone. Mind you she did me a treat. 'You can't take it with you!' Much they know. An annuity. Can you believe that? She was seven years older than me and she tied it all up in an annuity for her life."

He drank his wine down.

He muttered.

"The bitch."

SALMAN RUSHDIE

SALMAN RUSHDIE

Salman Rushdie was born in Bombay in 1947. He is a member of the production board of the British Film Institute, the advisory board of the Institute of Contemporary Arts and a Fellow of the Royal Society of Literature. He has in the past worked as a copywriter for the advertising agency Ogilvy and Mather. His previous works include *Grimus, Midnight's Children,* which won the 1981 Booker Prize, *Shame* (1983) and *The Satanic Verses* (1988) which were both shortlisted.

"Errata": or, Unreliable Narration in *Midnight's Children*

According to Hindu tradition, the elephant-headed god Ganesha is very fond of literature; so fond that he agrees to sit at the feet of the bard Vyasa and take down the entire text of the *Mahabharata*, from start to finish, in an unparalleled act of stenographic love.

In *Midnight's Children*, Saleem Sinai makes a reference, at one point, to this old tradition. But his version is a little different. According to Saleem, Ganesha sat at the feet of the poet Valmiki and took down the *Ramayana*. Saleem is wrong.

It is not his only mistake. During his account of the evolution of the city of Bombay, he tells us that the city's patron goddess Mumbadevi has fallen out of favour with contemporary Bombayites: "The calendar of festivals reveals her decline . . . where is Mumbadevi's day?" As a matter of fact, the calendar of festivals includes a perfectly good Mumbadevi Day, or, at least, it does in all versions of India except Saleem's.

And how could Lata Mangeshkar have been heard singing on All–India Radio as early as 1946? And does Saleem not know that it was not General Sam Manekshaw who accepted the surrender of the Pakistan Army at the end of the Bangladesh War – the Indian officer who was Tiger Niazi's old chum being, of course, Jagjit Singh Arora? And why does Saleem allege that the brand of cigarettes, State Express 555, is manufactured by W. D. and H. O. Wills?

I could continue. Concrete tetrapods have never been used in Bombay as part of any land reclamation scheme, but only to shore up and protect the sea wall along the Marine Drive promenade. Nor could the train that brings Picture Singh and

Saleem from Delhi to Bombay possibly have passed through Kurla, which is on a different line.

Et cetera. It is by now obvious, I hope, that Saleem Sinai is an unreliable narrator, and that *Midnight's Children* is far from being an authoritative guide to the history of post-independence India.

But this isn't quite how unreliable narration usually works in novels. Conventionally unreliable narrators are often a little stupid, less able to work out what's going on around them than the reader. In such narratives, one deciphers the true meaning of events by "seeing through" the narrator's faulty vision. However, the narrator of *Midnight's Children* is neither particularly stupid, nor particularly unaware of what's happening.

Why, then, all the errata? One answer could be that the author has been sloppy in his research. "If you're going to use Hindu traditions in your story, Mr Rushdie," I was asked by an irate and shiny-headed gentleman in Bangalore – he had spotted the Valmiki/Vyasa confusion – "don't you think you could take the trouble to look it up?" I have also received letters arguing about Bombay bus routes, and informing me that certain ranks used by the Pakistan Army in the text are not in fact used by the Pakistan Army in Pakistan. In these letters there is always an undertone of pleasure: the reader's delight at having "caught the writer out".

So let me confess that the novel does contain a few mistakes that are mine as well as Saleem's. One is to be found in the description of the Amritsar massacre, during which I have Saleem say that Dyer entered the Jallianwala Bagh compound followed by "fifty white troops". The truth is that there were fifty troops, but they weren't white. When I first found out my error I was upset and tried to have it corrected. Now I'm not so sure. The mistake feels more and more like Saleem's; its wrongness feels *right*.

Elsewhere, though, I went to some trouble to get things wrong. Originally error-free passages had the taint of inaccuracy introduced. Unintentional mistakes were, on being discovered, not expunged from the text but, rather, emphasised, given more prominence in the story. This odd behaviour requires an explanation.

When I began the novel (as I've written elsewhere) my purpose was somewhat Proustian. Time and migration had placed a double filter between me and my subject, and I hoped that if I could only imagine vividly enough it might be possible to see beyond those filters, to write as if the years had not passed, as if I had never left India for the West. But as I worked I found that what interested me was the process of filtration itself. So my subject changed, was no longer a search for lost time, had become the way in which we remake the past to suit our present purposes, using memory as our tool. Saleem's greatest desire is for what he calls meaning, and near the end of his broken life he sets out to write himself, in the hope that by doing so he may achieve the significance that the events of his adulthood have drained from him. He is no dispassionate, disinterested chronicler. He wants so to shape his material that the reader will be forced to concede his central role. He is cutting up history to suit himself, just as he did when he cut up newspapers to compose his earlier text, the anonymous note to Commander Sabarmati. The small errors in the text can be read as clues, as indications that Saleem is capable of distortions both great and small. He is an interested party in the events he narrates.

He is also *remembering*, of course, and one of the simplest truths about any set of memories is that many of them will be false. I myself have a clear memory of having been in India during the China war. I "remember" how frightened we all were, I "recall" people making nervy little jokes about needing to buy themselves a Chinese phrase-book or two, because the Chinese Army was not expected to stop until it reached Delhi. I also know that I could not possibly have been in India at that time. I was interested to find that *even after I found out that my memory was playing tricks* my brain simply refused to unscramble itself. It clung to the false memory, preferring it to mere, literal happenstance. I thought that was an important lesson to learn.

Thereafter, as I wrote the novel, and whenever a conflict arose between literal and remembered truth, I would favour the remembered version. This is why, even though Saleem admits that no tidal wave passed through the Sundarbans in the year of the Bangladesh War, he continues to be borne out of the jungle on the crest of that fictional wave. His truth is too important to him to allow it to be unseated by a mere weather report. It is memory's truth, he insists, and only a madman would prefer someone else's version to his own.

Saleem Sinai is not an oracle; he's only adopting a kind of oracular language. His story is not history, but it plays with historical shapes. Ironically, the book's success – its Booker, etc. – initially distorted the way in which it was read. Many readers wanted it to be the history, even the guide-book, which it was never meant to be; some others resented it for its incompleteness, pointing out, among other things, that I had failed to mention the glories of Urdu poetry; or the plight of the Harijans or untouchables; or what some people think of as the new imperialism of the Hindi language in South India. These variously disappointed readers were judging the book not as a novel, but as some sort of inadequate reference book or encyclopaedia.

The passage of time has smoothed out such wrinkles. I'd just like to clear up that mistake of Saleem's about the god Ganesha. It happens just after Saleem has been boasting about his own erudition. In spite of coming from a Muslim background, he tells us, he's well up on the Hindu stories. That he should instantly perpetrate a howler about the myth which is, after all, most central to himself (Ganesha's elephantine nose, and dubious parentage, prefigure his own), was, I thought, a way of deflating that narratorial pomposity; but it was also – along with Saleem's other blunder about the date of Mahatma Gandhi's assassination – a way of telling the reader to maintain a healthy distrust.

History is always ambiguous. Facts are hard to establish, and capable of being given many meanings. Reality is built on our prejudices, misconceptions and ignorance as well as on our perceptiveness and knowledge. The reading of Saleem's unreliable narration might be, I believed, a useful analogy for the way in which we all, every day, attempt to "read" the world.

Extract from *Midnight's Children*

Love in Bombay

During Ramzàn, the month of fasting, we went to the movies as often as we could. After being shaken awake at five a.m. by my mother's assiduous hand; after pre-dawn breakfasts of melon and sugared lime-water, and especially on Sunday mornings, the Brass Monkey and I took it in turns (or sometimes called out in unison) to remind Amina: "The ten-thirty-in-the-morning show! It's Metro Cub Club day, Amma, pleeeese!" Then the drive in the Rover to the cinema where we would taste neither Coca-Cola nor potato crisps, neither Kwality ice-cream nor samosas in greasy paper; but at least there was air-conditioning, and Cub Club badges pinned to our clothes, and competitions, and birthday-announcements made by a compère with an inadequate moustache; and finally, the film, after the trailers with their introductory titles, "Next Attraction" and "Coming Soon", and the cartoon ("In A Moment, The Big Film; But First . . . !"): *Quentin Durward*, perhaps, or *Scaramouche*. "Swashbuckling!" we'd say to one another afterwards, playing movie critic; and, "A rumbustious, bawdy romp!" – although we were ignorant of swashbuckles and bawdiness. There was not much praying in our family (except on Eid-ul-Fitr, when my father took me to the Friday mosque to celebrate the holiday by tying a handkerchief around my head and pressing my forehead to the ground) . . . but we were always willing to fast, because we liked the cinema.

Evie Burns and I agreed: the world's greatest movie star was Robert Taylor. I also liked Jay Silverheels as Tonto; but his kemosabay, Clayton Moore, was too fat for the Lone Ranger, in my view.

Evelyn Lilith Burns arrived on New Year's Day, 1957, to take up residence with her widower father in an apartment in one of the two squat, ugly concrete blocks which had grown up, almost without our noticing them, on the lower reaches of our hillock, and which were oddly segregated: Americans and other foreigners lived (like Evie) in Noor Ville; *arriviste* Indian success-stories ended up in Laxmi Vilas. From the heights of Methwold's Estate, we looked down on them all, on white and brown alike; but nobody ever looked down on Evie Burns – except once. Only once did anyone get on top of her.

Before I climbed into my first pair of long pants, I fell in love with Evie; but love was a curious, chain-reactive thing that year. To save time, I shall place all of us in the same row at the Metro cinema; Robert Taylor is mirrored in our eyes as we sit in flickering trances – and also in symbolic sequence: Saleem Sinai is sitting-next-to-and-in-love-with Evie Burns who is sitting-next-to-and-in-love-with Sonny Ibrahim who is sitting-next-to-and-in-love-with the Brass Monkey who is sitting next to the aisle and feeling starving hungry . . . I loved Evie for perhaps six months of my life; two years later, she was back in America, knifing an old woman and being sent to reform school.

A brief expression of my gratitude is in order at this point: if Evie had not come to live amongst us, my story might never have progressed beyond tourism-in-a-clocktower and cheating in class . . . and then there would have been no climax in a widows' hostel, no clear proof of my meaning, no coda in a fuming factory over which there presides the winking, saffron-and-green dancing figure of the neon goddess Mumbadevi. But Evie Burns (was she snake or ladder? The answer's obvious: *both*) did come, complete with the silver bicycle which enabled me not only to discover the midnight children, but also to ensure the partition of the state of Bombay.

To begin at the beginning: her hair was made of scarecrow straw, her skin was peppered with freckles and her teeth lived in a metal cage. These teeth were, it seemed, the only things on earth over which she was powerless – they grew wild, in malicious crazy-paving overlaps, and stung her dreadfully when she ate ice-cream. (I permit myself this one generalisation:

Americans have mastered the universe, but have no dominion over their mouths; whereas India is impotent, but her children tend to have excellent teeth.)

Racked by toothaches, my Evie rose magnificently above the pain. Refusing to be ruled by bone and gums, she ate cake and drank Coke whenever they were going; and never complained. A tough kid, Evie Burns: her conquest of suffering confirmed her sovereignty over us all. It has been observed that all Americans need a frontier: pain was hers, and she was determined to push it out.

Once, I shyly gave her a necklace of flowers (queen-of-the-night for my lily-of-the-eve), bought with my own pocket-money from a hawker-woman at Scandal Point. "I don't wear flowers," Evelyn Lilith said, and tossed the unwanted chain into the air, spearing it before it fell with a pellet from her unerring Daisy air-pistol. Destroying flowers with a Daisy, she served notice that she was not to be manacled, not even by a necklace: she was our capricious, whirligig Lill-of-the-Hill. And also Eve. The Adam's-apple of my eye.

How she arrived: Sonny Ibrahim, Eyeslice and Hairoil Sabarmati, Cyrus Dubash, the Monkey and I were playing French cricket in the circus-ring between Methwold's four palaces. A New Year's Day game: Toxy clapping at her barred window; even Bi-Appah was in good humour and not, for once, abusing us. Cricket – even French cricket, and even when played by children – is a quiet game: peace anointed in linseed oil. The kissing of leather and willow; sprinkled applause; the occasional cry – "Shot! Shot, sir!" – "Ow*zatt*??" but Evie on her bicycle was having none of that.

"Hey, you! Alla you! Hey, whassamatter? You all deaf or what?"

I was batting (elegantly as Ranji, powerfully as Vinoo Mankad) when she charged up the hill on her two-wheeler, straw hair flying, freckles ablaze, mouth-metal flashing semaphore messages in the sunlight, a scarecrow astride a silver bullet . . . "Hey, you widda leaky nose! Stop watching the schoopid ball, ya crumb! I'll showya something worth watching!"

Impossible to picture Evie Burns without also conjuring up a bicycle; and not just any two-wheeler, but one of the last of the great old-timers, an Arjuna Indiabike in mint condition, with drop-handlebars wrapped in masking tape and five gears and a seat made of reccine cheetah-skin. And a silver frame (the colour, I don't need to tell you, of the Lone Ranger's horse) . . . slobby Eyeslice and neat Hairoil, Cyrus the genius and the Monkey, and Sonny Ibrahim and myself – the best of friends, the true sons of the Estate, its heirs by right of birth – Sonny with the slow innocence he had had ever since the forceps dented his brain and me with my dangerous secret knowledge – yes, all of us, future bullfighters and Navy chiefs and all, stood frozen in open-mouthed attitudes as Evie Burns began to ride her bike, fasterfasterfaster, around and around the edges of the circus-ring. "Lookit me now: watch me go, ya dummies!"

On and off the cheetah-seat, Evie performed. One foot on the seat, one leg stretched out behind her, she whirled around us; she built up speed and then did a headstand on the seat! She could straddle the front wheel, facing the rear, and work the pedals the wrong way round . . . gravity was her slave, speed her element, and we knew that a power had come among us, a witch on wheels, and the flowers of the hedgerows threw her petals, the dust of the circus-ring stood up in clouds of ovation, because the circus-ring had found its mistress, too: it was the canvas beneath the brush of her whirling wheels.

Now we noticed that our heroine packed a Daisy air-pistol on her right hip . . . "More to come, ya zeroes!" she yelled, and drew the weapon. Her pellets gave stones the gift of flight; we threw annas into the air and she gunned them down, stone-dead. "Targets! More targets!" – and Eyeslice surrendered his be-loved pack of rummy cards without a murmur, so that she could shoot the heads off the kings. Annie Oakley in tooth-braces – nobody dared question her sharpshooting, except once, and that was at the end of her reign, during the great cat invasion; and there were extenuating circumstances.

Flushed, sweating, Evie Burns dismounted and announced: "From now on, there's a new big chief around here. Okay, Indians? Any arguments?"

No arguments; I knew then that I had fallen in love.

At Juhu Beach with Evie: she won the camel-races, could drink more coconut milk than any of us, could open her eyes under the sharp salt water of the Arabian Sea.

Did six months make such a difference? (Evie was half a year older than me.) Did it entitle you to talk to grown-ups as an equal? Evie was seen gossiping with old man Ibrahim Ibrahim; she claimed Lila Sabarmati was teaching her to put on make-up; she visited Homi Catrack to gossip about guns. (It was the tragic irony of Homi Catrack's life that he, at whom a gun would one day be pointed, was a true *aficionado* of firearms . . . in Evie he found a fellow-creature, a motherless child who was, unlike his own Toxy, as sharp as a knife and as bright as a bottle. Incidentally, Evie Burns wasted no sympathy on poor Toxy Catrack. "Wrong inna head," she opined carelessly to us all, "Oughta be put down like rats." But Evie: rats are not weak! There was more that was rodent-like in your face than in the whole body of your despised Tox.)

That was Evelyn Lilith; and within weeks of her arrival, I had set off the chain reaction from whose effects I would never fully recover.

It began with Sonny Ibrahim, Sonny-next-door, Sonny of the forcep-hollows, who has been sitting patiently in the wings of my story, awaiting his cue. In those days, Sonny was a badly bruised fellow: more than forceps had dented him. To love the Brass Monkey (even in the nine-year-old sense of the word) was no easy thing to do.

As I've said, my sister, born second and unheralded, had begun to react violently to any declarations of affection. Although she was believed to speak the language of birds and cats, the soft words of lovers roused in her an almost animal rage; but Sonny was too simple to be warned off. For months now, he had been pestering her with statements such as, "Saleem's sister, you're a pretty solid type!" or, "Listen, you want to be my girl? We could go to the pictures with your ayah, maybe . . ." And for an equal number of months, she had been making him suffer for his love – telling tales to his mother; pushing him into mud-puddles accidentally-on-purpose; once even assaulting him physically, leaving him with long raking claw-marks down his face and an expression of sad-dog injury in his eyes; but he would not learn. And so, at last, she had planned her most terrible revenge.

The Monkey attended Walsingham School for Girls on Nepean Sea Road; a school full of tall, superbly muscled Europeans, who swam like fish and dived like submarines. In their spare time, they could be seen from our bedroom window, cavorting in the map-shaped pool of the Breach Candy Club, from which we were, of course, barred . . . and when I discovered that the Monkey had somehow attached herself to these segregated swimmers, as a sort of mascot, I felt genuinely aggrieved with her for perhaps the first time . . . but there was no arguing with her; she went her own way. Beefy fifteen-year-old white girls let her sit with them on the Walsingham school bus. Three such females would wait with her every morning at the same place where Sonny, Eyeslice, Hairoil, Cyrus-the-great and I awaited the bus from the Cathedral School.

One morning, for some forgotten reason, Sonny and I were the only boys at the stop. Maybe there was a bug going round or something. The Monkey waited until Mary Pereira had left us alone, in the care of the beefy swimmers; and then suddenly the truth of what she was planning flashed into my head as, for no particular reason, I tuned into her thoughts; and I yelled "Hey!" – but too late. The Monkey screeched, "You keep out of this!" and then she and the three beefy swimmers had jumped upon Sonny Ibrahim, street-sleepers and beggars and bicycling clerks were watching with open amusement, because they were ripping every scrap of clothing off his body . . . "Damn it man, are you going just to stand and watch?" – Sonny yelling for help, but I was immobilised, how could I take sides between my sister and my best friend, and he, "I'll tell my daddy on you!", tearful now, while the Monkey, "That'll teach you to talk shit – and that'll teach you," his shoes, off; no shirt any more; his vest, dragged off by a high-board diver, "And that'll teach you to write your sissy love letters," no socks now, and plenty of tears, and "There!" yelled the Monkey; the Walsingham bus arrived and the assailants and my sister jumped in and sped away, "Ta-ta-ba-ta, lover-boy!" they yelled, and Sonny was left in the street, on the pavement opposite Chimalker's and Reader's Paradise, naked as the day he was born; his forcep-hollows glistened like rock-pools, because Vaseline had dripped into them from his hair; and his eyes were wet as well, as he, "Why's she do it, man? Why, when I only told her I liked . . ."

"Search me," I said, not knowing where to look. "She does things, that's all." Not knowing, either, that the time would come when she did something worse to me.

But that was nine years later . . . meanwhile, early in 1957, election campaigns had begun: the Jan Sangh was campaigning for rest homes for aged sacred cows; in Kerala, E. M. S. Namboodiripad was promising that Communism would give everyone food and jobs; in Madras, the Anna-D.M.K. party of C. N. Annadurai fanned the flames of regionalism; the Congress fought back with reforms such as the Hindu Succession Act, which gave Hindu women equal rights of inheritance . . . in short, everybody was busy pleading his own cause; I, however, found myself tongue-tied in the face of Evie Burns, and approached Sonny Ibrahim to ask him to plead on my behalf.

In India, we've always been vulnerable to Europeans . . . Evie had only been with us a matter of weeks, and already I was being sucked into a grotesque mimicry of European literature. (We had done *Cyrano*, in a simplified version, at school; I had also read the *Classics Illustrated* comic book.) Perhaps it would be fair to say that Europe repeats itself, in India, as farce . . . Evie was American. Same thing.

"But hey, man, that's no-fair man, why don't you do it yourself?"

"Listen, Sonny," I pleaded, "you're my friend, right?"

"Yeah, but you didn't even help . . ."

"That was my sister, Sonny, so how could I?"

"No, so you have to do your own dirty . . ."

"Hey, Sonny, man, think. Think only. These girls need careful handling, man. Look how the Monkey flies off the handle! You've got the experience, yaar, you've been through it. You'll know how to go gently this time. What do I know, man? Maybe she doesn't like me even. You want me to have my clothes torn off, too? That would make you feel better?"

And innocent, good-natured Sonny, ". . . Well, no . . ."

"Okay, then. You go. Sing my praises a little. Say never mind about my nose. Character is what counts. You can do that?"

". . . Weeeelll . . . I . . . okay, but you talk to your sis also, yah?"

"I'll talk, Sonny. What can I promise? You know what she's like. But I'll talk to her for sure."

You can lay your strategies as carefully as you like, but women will undo them at a stroke. For every victorious election campaign, there are twice as many that fail . . . from the verandah of Buckingham Villa, through the slats of the chick-blind, I spied on Sonny Ibrahim as he canvassed my chosen constituency . . . and heard the voice of the electorate, the rising nasality of Evie Burns, splitting the air with scorn: "Who? *Him?* Whynt'cha tell him to jus' go blow his nose? That sniffer? He can't even ride a *bike*!"

Which was true.

And there was worse to come; because now (although a chick-blind divided the scene into narrow slits) did I not see the expression on Evie's face begin to soften and change? – did Evie's hand (sliced lengthways by the chick) not reach out towards my electoral agent? – and weren't those Evie's fingers (the nails bitten down to the quick) touching Sonny's temple-hollows, the fingertips getting covered in dribbled Vaseline? – and did Evie say or did she not: "Now you, f'r instance: you're *cute*"? Let me sadly affirm that I did; it did; they were; she did.

Saleem Sinai loves Evie Burns; Evie loves Sonny Ibrahim; Sonny is potty about the Brass Monkey; but what does the Monkey say?

"Don't make me sick, Allah," my sister said when I tried – rather nobly, considering how he'd failed me – to argue Sonny's case. The voters had given the thumbs-down to us both.

I wasn't giving in just yet. The siren temptations of Evie Burns – who never cared about me, I'm bound to admit – led me inexorably towards my fall. (But I hold nothing against her; because my fall led to a rise.)

Privately, in my clocktower, I took time off my trans-subcontinental rambles to consider the wooing of my freckled Eve. "Forget middle-men," I advised myself. "You'll have to do this personally." Finally, I formed my scheme: I would have to share her interests, to make her passions mine . . . guns have never appealed to me. I resolved to learn how to ride a bike.

Evie, in those days, had given in to the many demands of the hillock-top children that she teach them her bicycle-arts; so it was a simple matter for me to join the queue for lessons. We assembled in the circus-ring; Evie, ring-mistress supreme, stood in the centre of five wobbly, furiously concentrating cyclists . . . while I stood beside her, bikeless. Until Evie's coming I'd shown no interest in wheels, so I'd never been given any . . . humbly, I suffered the lash of Evie's tongue.

"Where've you been *living*, fat nose? I suppose you wanna borrow mine?"

"No," I lied penitently, and she relented. "Okay, okay," Evie shrugged, "Get in the saddle and lessee whatchou're made of."

Let me reveal at once that, as I climbed on to the silver Arjuna Indiabike, I was filled with the purest elation; that, as Evie walked roundandround, holding the bike by the handlebars, exclaiming, "Gotcha balance yet? *No?* Geez, nobody's got all year!" – as Evie and I perambulated, I felt . . . what's the word? . . . happy.

Roundandroundand . . . Finally, to please her, I stammered, "Okay . . . I think I'm . . . let me," and instantly I was on my own, she had given me a farewell shove, and the silver creature flew gleaming and uncontrollable across the circus-ring . . . I heard her shouting: "The brake! Use the goddamn brake, ya dummy!" – but my hands couldn't move, I had gone rigid as a plank, and there LOOK OUT in front of me was the blue two-wheeler of Sonny Ibrahim, collision course, OUTA THE WAY YA CRAZY, Sonny in the saddle, trying to swerve and miss, but still blue streaked towards silver, Sonny swung right but I went the same way EEYAH MY BIKE and silver wheel touched blue, frame kissed frame, I was flying up and over handlebars towards Sonny who had embarked on an identical parabola towards me CRASH bicycles fell to earth beneath us, locked in an intimate embrace CRASH suspended in mid-air Sonny and I met each other, Sonny's head

greeted mine . . . Over nine years ago I had been born with
bulging temples, and Sonny had been given hollows by forceps;
everything is for a reason, it seems, because now my bulging
temples found their way into Sonny's hollows. A perfect fit.
Heads fitting together, we began our descent to earth, falling
clear of the bikes, fortunately, WHUMMP and for a moment the
world went away.

Then Evie with her freckles on fire, "O ya little creep, ya pile
of snot, ya wrecked my . . ." But I wasn't listening, because
circus-ring accident had completed what washing-chest calamity
had begun, and they were there in my head, in the front now,
no longer a muffled background noise I'd never noticed, all of
them, sending their here-I-am signals, from north south east
west . . . the other children born during that midnight hour,
calling "I", "I", "I" and "I."

"Hey! Hey, snothead! You okay? . . . Hey, where's his
mother?"

Interruptions, nothing but interruptions! The different parts of
my somewhat complicated life refuse, with a wholly unreason-
able obstinacy, to stay neatly in their separate compartments.
Voices spill out of their clocktower to invade the circus-ring,
which is supposed to be Evie's domain . . . and now, at the very
moment when I should be describing the fabulous children of
ticktock, I'm being whisked away by Frontier Mail – spirited off
to the decaying world of my grandparents, so that Aadam Aziz
is getting in the way of the natural unfolding of my tale. Ah well.
What can't be cured must be endured.

That January, during my convalescence from the severe
concussion I received in my bicycling accident, my parents took
us off to Agra for a family reunion that turned out worse than
the notorious (and arguably fictional) Black Hole of Calcutta. For
two weeks we were obliged to listen to Emerald and Zulfikar
(who was now a Major-General and insisted on being called a
General) dropping names, and also hints of their fabulous wealth,
which had by now grown into the seventh largest private fortune
in Pakistan; their son Zafar tried (but only once!) to pull the
Monkey's fading red pig-tails. And we were obliged to watch in

silent horror while my Civil Servant uncle Mustapha and his half-Irani wife Sonia beat and bludgeoned their litter of nameless, genderless brats into utter anonymity; and the bitter aroma of Alia's spinsterhood filled the air and ruined our food; and my father would retire early to begin his secret nightly war against the djinns; and worse, and worse, and worse.

One night I awoke on the stroke of twelve to find my grandfather's dream inside my head, and was therefore unable to avoid seeing him as he saw himself – as a crumbling old man in whose centre, when the light was right, it was possible to discern a gigantic shadow. As the convictions which had given strength to his youth withered away under the combined influence of old age, Reverend Mother and the absence of likeminded friends, an old hole was reappearing in the middle of his body, turning him into just another shrivelled, empty old man, over whom the God (and other superstitions) against which he'd fought for so long was beginning to reassert His dominion . . . meanwhile, Reverend Mother spent the entire fortnight finding little ways of insulting my uncle Hanif's despised film-actress wife. And that was also the time when I was cast as a ghost in a children's play, and found, in an old leather attaché-case on top of my grandfather's almirah, a sheet which had been chewed by moths, but whose largest hole was man-made: for which discovery I was repaid (you will recall) in roars of grandparental rage.

But there was one achievement. I was befriended by Rashid the rickshaw-wallah (the same fellow who had, in his youth, screamed silently in a cornfield and helped Nadir Khan into Aadam Aziz's toilet): taking me under his wing – and without telling my parents, who would have forbidden it so soon after my accident – he taught me how to ride a bicycle. By the time we left, I had this secret tucked away with all my others: only I didn't intend this one to stay secret for very long.

. . . And on the train home, there were voices hanging on to the outside of the compartment: "Ohé, maharaj! Open up, great sir!" – fare-dodgers' voices fighting with the ones I wanted to listen to, the new ones inside my head – and then back to Bombay Central Station, and the drive home past racecourse and temple, and now Evelyn Lilith Burns is demanding that I finish her part first before concentrating on higher things.

"Home again!" the Monkey shouts. "Hurray . . . Back-to-Bom!" (She is in disgrace. In Agra, she incinerated the General's boots.)

It is a matter of record that the States Reorganisation Committee had submitted its report to Mr Nehru as long ago as October 1955; a year later, its recommendations had been implemented. India had been divided anew, into fourteen states and six centrally-administered "territories". But the boundaries of these states were not formed by rivers, or mountains, or any natural features of the terrain; they were, instead, walls of words. Language divided us: Kerala was for speakers of Malayalam, the only palindromically-named tongue on earth; in Karnataka you were supposed to speak Kanarese; and the amputated state of Madras – known today as Tamil Nadu – enclosed the *aficionados* of Tamil. Owing to some oversight, however, nothing was done with the state of Bombay; and in the city of Mumbadevi, the language marches grew longer and noisier and finally metamorphosed into political parties, the Samyukta Maharashtra Samiti ("United Maharashtra Party") which stood for the Marathi language and demanded the creation of the Deccan state of Maharashtra, and the Maha Gujarat Parishad ("Great Gujarat Party") which marched beneath the banner of the Gujarati language and dreamed of a state to the north of Bombay City, stretching all the way to the Kathiawar peninsula and the Rann of Kutch . . . I am warming over all this cold history, these old dead struggles between the barren angularity of Marathi which was born in the arid heat of the Deccan and Gujarati's boggy, Kathiawari softness, to explain why, on the day in February 1957 immediately following our return from Agra, Methwold's Estate was cut off from the city by a stream of chanting humanity which flooded Warden Road more completely than monsoon water, a parade so long that it took two days to pass, and of which it was said that the statue of Sivaji had come to life to ride stonily at its head. The demonstrators carried black flags; many of them were shopkeepers on hartal; many were striking textile-workers from Mazagaon and Matunga; but on our hillock, we knew nothing about their jobs; to us children, the endless ant-trail of language in Warden Road seemed as magnetically fascinating as a light-bulb to a moth. It was a demonstration so immense, so intense in its passions, that it made all previous marches vanish from the mind as if they had never occurred – and we had all been banned from going down the hill for even the tiniest of looks. So who was the boldest of us all? Who urged us to creep at least half-way down, to the point where the hillock-road swung round to face Warden Road in a steep U-bend? Who said, "What's to be scared of? We're only going half-way for a *peek*"? . . . Wide-eyed, disobedient Indians followed their freckled American chief. ("They killed Dr Narlikar – marchers did," Hairoil warned us in a shivery voice. Evie spat on his shoes.)

But I, Saleem Sinai, had other fish to fry. "Evie," I said with quiet offhandedness, "how'd you like to see me bicycling?" No response. Evie was immersed in the spectacle . . . and was that her fingerprint in Sonny Ibrahim's left forcep-hollow, embedded in Vaseline for all the world to see? A second time, and with slightly more emphasis, I said, "I can do it, Evie. I'll do it on the Monkey's cycle. You want to watch?" And now Evie, cruelly, "I'm watching this. This is good. Why'd I wanna watch *you*?" And me, a little snivelly now, "But I *learned*, Evie, you've *got* to . . ." Roars from Warden Road below us drown my words. Her back is to me; and Sonny's back, the backs of Eyeslice and Hairoil, the intellectual rear of Cyrus-the-great . . . my sister, who has seen the fingerprint too, and looks displeased, eggs me on: "Go on. Go on, show her. Who's she think she is?" And up on her bike . . . "I'm doing it, Evie, look!" Bicycling in circles, round and round the little cluster of children, "See? You *see*?" A moment of exultation; and then Evie, deflating impatient couldn't-care-less; "Willya get outa my way, fer Petesake? I wanna see *that*!" Finger, chewed-off nail and all, jabs down in the direction of the language march; I am dismissed in favour of the parade of the Samyukta Maharashtra Samiti! And despite the Monkey, who loyally, "That's not fair! He's doing it really *good*!" – and in spite of the exhilaration of the thing-in-itself –

something goes haywire inside me; and I'm riding round Evie, fasterfasterfaster, crying sniffing out of control, "So what is it with you, anyway? What do I have to do to . . ." And then something else takes over, because I realise I don't have to ask her, I can just get inside that freckled mouth-metalled head and find out, for once I can really get to know what's going on . . . and in I go, still bicycling, but the front of her mind is all full up with Marathi language-marchers, there are American pop songs stuck in the corners of her thoughts, but nothing I'm interested in; and now, only now, now for the very first time, now driven on by the tears of unrequited love, I begin to probe . . . I find myself pushing, diving, forcing my way behind her defences . . . into the secret place where there's a picture of her mother who wears a pink smock and holds up a tiny fish by the tail, and I'm ferreting deeperdeeperdeeper, where is it, what makes her tick, when she gives a sort of jerk and swings round to stare at me as I bicycle roundandroundandroundandroundand . . .

"Get out!" screams Evie Burns. Hands lifted to forehead. I bicycling, wet-eyed, diving ininin: to where Evie stands in the doorway of a clapboard bedroom holding a, holding a something sharp and glinty with red dripping off it, in the doorway of a, my God and on the bed a woman, who, in a pink, my God, and Evie with the, and red staining the pink, and a man coming, my God, and no no no no no . . .

"GET OUT GET OUT GET OUT!" Bewildered children watch as Evie screams, language march forgotten, but suddenly remembered again, because Evie has grabbed the back of the Monkey's bike WHAT'RE YOU DOING EVIE as she pushes it THERE GET OUT YA BUM THERE GET OUT TO HELL! — She's pushed me hard-as-hard, and I losing control hurtling down the slope round the end of the U-bend downdown, MY GOD THE MARCH past Band Box laundry, past Noor Ville and Laxmi Vilas, AAAAA and down into the mouth of the march, heads feet bodies, the waves of the march parting as I arrive, yelling blue murder, crashing into history on a runaway, young-girl's bike.

Hands grabbing handlebars as I slow down in the impassioned throng. Smiles filled with good teeth surround me. They are not friendly smiles. "Look look, a little laad-sahib comes down to

join us from the big rich hill!" In Marathi which I hardly understand, it's my worst subject at school, and the smiles asking,
"You want to join S.M.S., little princeling?" And I, just about
knowing what's being said, but dazed into telling the truth, shake
my head No. And the smiles, "Oho! The young nawab does not
like our tongue! What does he like?" And another smile, "Maybe
Gujarati! You speak Gujarati, my lord?" But my Gujarati was as
bad as my Marathi; I only knew one thing in the marshy tongue
of Kathiawar; and the smiles, urging, and the fingers, prodding,
"Speak, little master! Speak some Gujarati!" – so I told them
what I knew, a rhyme I'd learned from Glandy Keith Colaco at
school, which he used when he was bullying Gujarati boys; a
rhyme designed to make fun of the speech rhythms of the
language:

> *Soo ché? Saru ché!*
> *Danda lé ké maru ché!*

*How are you? – I am well! – I'll take a stick and thrash you to
hell!* A nonsense; a nothing; nine words of emptiness . . . but
when I'd recited them, the smiles began to laugh; and then
voices near me and then further and further away began to take
up my chant, HOW ARE YOU? I AM WELL!, and they lost interest in
me, "Go go with your bicycle, masterji," they scoffed, I'LL TAKE
A STICK AND THRASH YOU TO HELL, I fled away up the hillock as my
chant rushed forward and back, up to the front and down to the
back of the two-day-long procession, becoming, as it went, a
song of war.

That afternoon, the head of the procession of the Samyukta
Maharashtra Samiti collided at Kemp's Corner, with the head of
a Maha Gujarat Parishad demonstration; S.M.S. voices chanted
"Soo ché? Saru ché?" and M.G.P. throats were opened in fury;
under the posters of the Air-India rajah and of the Kolynos Kid,
the two parties fell upon one another with no little zeal, and to
the tune of my little rhyme the first of the language riots got
under way, fifteen killed, over three hundred wounded.

In this way I became directly responsible for triggering off
the violence which ended with the partition of the state of

Bombay, as a result of which the city became the capital of Maharashtra – so at least I was on the winning side.

What was it in Evie's head? Crime or dream? I never found out; but I had learned something else: when you go deep inside someone's head, *they can feel you in there.*

Evelyn Lilith Burns didn't want much to do with me after that day; but strangely enough, I was cured of her. (Women have always been the ones to change my life: Mary Pereira, Evie Burns, Jamila Singer, Parvati-the-witch must answer for who I am; and the Widow, who I'm keeping for the end; and after the end, Padma, my goddess of dung. Women have fixed me all right, but perhaps they were never central – perhaps the place which they should have filled, the hole in the centre of me which was my inheritance from my grandfather Aadam Aziz, was occupied for too long by my voices. Or perhaps – one must consider all possibilities – they always made me a little afraid.)

THOMAS KENEALLY

THOMAS KENEALLY

Thomas Keneally began writing in 1964. His novels include *The Chant of Jimmie Blacksmith, Confederates* and *Gossip from the Forest,* each shortlisted for the Booker Prize, as well as *Schindler's Ark* which won the Booker Prize in 1982.

His most recent novels are *The Playmaker* and *Towards Asmara* (1989). He is also the author of *Outback,* an account of life in Central Australia (1983). Born in northern New South Wales in 1935, he now lives in Sydney with his wife. They have two daughters.

This is a segment from a novel I have never finished, a novel about an Australian Candide travelling in Poland during Solidarity's last summer, before the brutality of martial law descended. The incidents and the tone of the piece are based on the journey I made to Poland myself in 1981 to do research for the book which would become *Schindler's Ark*, controversial winner of the 1982 Booker Prize.

I chose this piece because it has to do with the continuity of tyranny and the parallel continuity of hope. Despite their grievous history, the Poles were a radiant people that spring and summer of 1981. The food queues were long, the housing squalid, the surveillance of the police state continuous, yet the fervour and expectation of the people were intoxicating to the spirit. Moving through Warsaw and Kracow streets rendered sinister by the modern subtleties of modern oppression, I was researching an earlier despotism – that of the Nazi occupation of 1939–45. I travelled with a Polish–American like Edek Kempner and a cab driver who knew of Walesa, and learned that it is in slits in sun visors that the face of human dignity often must be hidden.

You don't know what in the hell I mean? Well, gentle reader, all will be revealed.

I have to say it: *Schindler's Ark* won the Booker – through some blessed aberration on the part of the judges – the year after Salman Rushdie's *Midnight's Children* did. The small chapter here presented – with its intimations of threat – reminds me of Rushdie, and of how he was in the days before threat, on Booker night 1982, this dinner-suited literary champion who sat at ease in Stationers' Hall, already a winner.

Recently, at a New York rally in honour of his life and right of free expression, I was handed the poster I was to carry. It said, "Long Live Rushdie." The one I would rather have got was the one given to the person next to me. "I Am Rushdie," it read. We all are, not in talent, but in solidarity (that good Polish word). In the fortunate solidarity of Booker laureates, may I dedicate this little piece to Salman.

The Man Who Knew Walesa

Polish officials and the troops at the airport wore a rich red kind of khaki and nifty little Kalashnikov automatic rifles. To meet this latter day Polish army, the old Polish warrior Edek Kempner wore his Orbis badge, the badge of the Polish Travel bureau, and on this afternoon of Polish crisis when the national blood was – as it were – rushing to Bydgoszcz where a farmer had been beaten up, the seas of Polish officialdom nonetheless parted before Edek and his party. "I said to that son-of-bitch in the uniform," Edek told his group, while doing business with two porters, one to handle Halinka's luggage, the other to tote that of the three men, "I tell that son-of-bitch that though I am American I do lots of work with the Orbis New York office. He asks me what's the address of the New York office. I flabbergast the boychick by telling him 500 Fifth Avenue. I even give him the zip code. He'll check. They check on everything. But Droz who runs the New York office will cover for his old friend Kempner, you better believe it." He winked, implying some long-standing deal between himself and this Droz, whom Clancy had never met. "One Pole can wash another Pole's hands."

They were funnelled through a last barrier. A vast crowd seemed to be waiting such a small trickle of passengers. "Most of them are probably spies," murmured Halinka, the flesh around her eyes having gone blue as if her homecoming had deprived her of oxygen.

And everyone was staring – at the good overcoats of Fodor and Edek, at Halinka's fur, even at the negligent but – by Eastern European norms – affluent clothing of Clancy, the jacket adequate by the standards of a Sydney winter but too thin for Poland, the polo neck Arran Isle sweater proof against most climates. And of course, they stared at Fodor, for on their soil there had been in the grievous early forties an attempt to expunge dwarfs. "Should I do a goddamn trick for them?" Fodor asked Clancy.

"Change US dollars in the car park, change US dollars in the car park," murmured a grey-faced man whom Clancy passed.

"Take no notice," Fodor advised. "The motherfucker could be an *agent provocateur*."

Edek, ahead with the porters, was pounced upon out of the crowd by a small man with a bald head and broad Slavic features, the sort of features Clancy was familiar with in Polish emigrants to Australia, the sort of face one saw, the features both hefty and hearty, on road workers, railway guards, cab drivers, in that far south land. Clancy knew it was always the peasants who were likely to travel furthest when they left their homelands – his own grandparents had been Irish peasants. The little ambusher was laughing and had begun to embrace Edek. Within an instant his affection was swallowed in the bear-like arms of Edouard of Beverly Hills. "You little son of gun," roared Edek. His expansiveness terrified some of the crowd this perilous evening and they moved away. Edek sprayed the terminal with affectionate Polish and the little man answered in a self-controlled way, in the way his blood, witness to so many generations of oppression, counselled him. Edek turned to the rest of his party and dragged them into a scrum with the small man he had just finished embracing. The small man was called Bogdan. He was a Warsaw cab driver to whose family Edek sent food parcels from that company in Chicago who made them up. He was a darling son of gun and would drive them all round Poland for a few hundred dollars, well maybe three hundred and fifty dollars, which he could then exchange on the open market for about three months' wages. *"Dobry wieczor,"* said Fodor and Halinka. Clancy tried the same subtle combination of vowels in greeting the cab driver, and Bogdan and his three fellow travellers laughed benignly. It occurred to Clancy, not for the first time, that Polish history – including that *outré* corner of it in which these people had acted – might be as subtle and unachievable to him as were the national vowels.

Outside, in the raw and strange air, Clancy was alarmed by a violent tug on his arm. Turning, he saw it was Halinka, baulked on the pavement. He became aware that her breath was rasping. Her lips parted and a small wail emerged. Bogdan was running merrily to fetch his cab, Edek yelling merrily in his wake and ordering the porters to halt and be patient. Halinka's talons on Clancy's arm seemed to penetrate his clothing. He hoped he could tow her, but to his amazement she held him static. The wail grew in volume. Fodor, on the other side of her, fetched her a sharp punch in the kidneys with his gloved hand. Clancy could hear that the blow cut off her breath. "Come on, sweetie," said Fodor. "No one can touch you. You're a free woman, a citizen of the right half of goddamn Germany."

Bogdan arrived in his cab, a Mercedes. A suitable vehicle, Clancy thought. Minute Bogdan lashed all Halinka's luggage on the roof rack. Fodor threw her in the back like a vice cop throwing a prostitute. As Clancy climbed in, she murmured at him, "Homecomings? I should not have come. They can sniff my Jewblood and they blame me for the crucified Pole that hangs in every Church."

"For what it's worth," said Clancy, taking her bird-like wrist, "You look like a Frankfurt woman or a New Yorker full stop." He knew that the Rist women had not been branded with a tattoo in Auschwitz – they had not been considered permanent enough residents for such treatment. His research told him, too, that when the Jews first came to Kazinierz in Kracow in the fourteenth century, they had resembled the Bedouin, and that only generations of *sub rosa* couplings had made her look so international and Edek look so Polish.

Edek had entered the back of the limo now and taken up the burden of consolation. "Don't you worry about a thing, darling. You are with Uncle Edek now. One mention of the US Consul and they shit themselves. Believe me, I know the set-up." He clapped his hands and beamed at Clancy, Fodor, Halinka. "This is fun! Poland in the spring!"

So they rolled through high-rise suburbs, Clancy looking for signs of the Polish anguish. He pointed to a vast hoarding on one apartment building. "What does it say?" he asked Edek.

Edek translated. *"The parish of Muranow welcomes the Virgin Mary.* It's a statue, Clancy. It moves around from parish to parish."

Clancy thought of the time he had walked three miles in Western Sydney to see Father Peyton's statue of the Virgin. The universality of Catholic culture! The foot of the Virgin crushing the serpent both in Warsaw Province and in distant New South Wales.

A public park appeared. "I performed there once," said Fodor. "August of '38. That's when circuses were circuses. People had an honest attitude to freaks. Hitler changed all that. People don't feel comfortable about us any more. I did the stilt act here. Come in on stilts dressed as a member of the goddamn Hapsburg family. Throw off the crown, throw off the ermine, jump off the stilts, and people gasp. What they thought was a prince is a midget. They were the days!"

"Higher wages for higher production," Edek translated a notice on an overhead bridge. But then Mariology reasserted itself. *"Oh Glorious Virgin, we your servants in Wilanow greet you with love,"* proclaimed a banner draped from a construction crane.

"This little fellow," laughed Edek, reaching through to the front seat and tweaking the ear of Bogdan, "he knows Walesa. He knows Klasa in Kracow – you know, Urek Klasa, Walesa's lieutenant down there in my old stamping grounds, my home-town. And he knows Wajda the movie maker and he knows Roman Polanski, that son-of-bitch who does things with children and he knows the other movie maker, the Kracow man, Blumen-tal, who is a Jew – I used to walk out with his aunt and take her to goddamn patisseries, would you believe?"

Bogdan smiled over his shoulder. Clancy wondered whether it *was* possible that he knew Walesa and the elfin Polanski and Blumental whose film on an electrician's family struggling for economic and spiritual space in one of the suburbs of Kracow had been a hit at festivals in the West.

As if at Edek's invitation, Bogdan the cab driver began talking fiercely. Clancy noticed how intently Fodor and even the barely restored Halinka were listening. Occasionally Edek's *basso* would intrude, a brief translation session for the sake of the Australian.

It happened that in the mid 1970s when Bogdan was young and newly married, he had found himself living in the same Gdansk apartment block as Walesa and Walesa's wife and children. He had lost his job as a toolmaker more or less at the same time as Walesa the electrician was sacked by the works committee. He had moved to Warsaw, his wife's city, and taken up with the cab business. It was the best move he could have made, he said (as translated by Edek). You met foreigners who left novels behind in the car – American novels, French novels, novels which delighted his daughter who was training to be a teacher. The other thing the Americans and the West Germans had was a strong currency, but you met Japanese too. The Japanese were wonderful, said Bogdan. They did things in real style and their generosity earned them top marks with Warsaw cab drivers. Not that there was anything wrong with Americans. Americans had top marks too.

Bogdan struck Clancy therefore as a revolutionary neutralised somewhat by contact with the right currencies. Clancy surmised too that nearly everyone in Poland, exclusive of certain security forces and Party die-hards, was claiming a connection with the phenomenon Walesa. As if to answer this suspicion, Bogdan flipped the sun visor above his head downwards – cab drivers often carried their treasures stuck on the underside of sun visors with an elastic band. Bogdan extracted a photograph, however, not from the underside but from a cunning slit in the leather. He pushed the photograph over his shoulder and towards Clancy in the back seat. Clancy examined it. It was a colour photograph some years old, an indoor shot, and the tile stove, living-room wall and other background, including a framed print of the Sacred Heart of Jesus, had taken on a coppery tint as if oxidised by all the reverent hands which touched it. There were two youngish and anciently Slavic women in the photograph, a younger Bogdan with more hair, and the unmistakable square features and droopy moustache of a young Lech Walesa. "Lescek live at apartment five," Bogdan explained. "I live at apartment seven. One . . . *ktorym . . .*"

He gestured upwards with an index finger. Edek again tweaked the driver's cheek. "This gorgeous little guy lived one floor up from Walesa." He began grilling Bogdan in Polish and conveying the information to Clancy. "The photograph is 1972. Bogdan and Walesa represented the same work section on the workers' council at the shipyard. Did you see his little wife in the photograph? She's adorable!" *Adorable* was an adjective to which Edek gave a luscious emphasis, pronouncing the second syllable *doo-er*.

Bogdan continued to tell his story in Polish. Edek Kempner continued to translate. Bogdan had worked as a welder in the transport section of the shipyards, a fairly remote depot out near the Dead Vistula to which they sent troublemakers. Walesa had been an electrician, Bogdan a welder side-tracked to delivering truck engines to some further workshop in that enormous industrial region. One day in the autumn of '78 the management had told the works council that Lech Walesa had to go. The workshop manager did his best to stand up for Lech but knew it was his job too on the line. The section supervisor refused to act on the dismissal and was demoted to become a storeman. A week later Bogdan and another Walesa lieutenant were sacked. (Edek conveyed all this with plentiful reference to son-of-bitch tyrants.)

It is hard enough being on a skilled worker's wage in Poland, Edek translated. To be unemployed is madness and hell.

Clancy imagined a bleak Baltic industrial-scape, a milieu bearable only if one were relating to it with a welding torch, a rivetting gun, or the controls of a crane. Bogdan said Walesa was unabashed by his dismissal. He went on sticking up posters, and when an engineer at the Siennecka Street workshops tore down one of them and then was later injured by a turbine engine which fell out of its tackle, Lescek visited the man in hospital and said, "God punished you, because we put the truth up on the wall and you tore it down. Don't tear down the truth again!"

Bogdan confessed through his interpreter Edek that he himself did not have such certainty about the direct hand of God in Polish affairs. His sacking had frightened the stuffing out of him. God and His Blessed Mother were to be thanked for Bogdan's father-in-law, whom until then Bogdan had considered something of a social parasite, a Warsaw dealer who seemed to be able to travel to West Germany frequently and take plenty of Carmel cigarettes with him. The Polish cigarette had for some reason always had a vogue in Western Europe – now more so than ever due to Lescek's international popularity, no matter how misunderstood Lescek might be on the international scene. I mean, Lescek is a Pole. He is not some Hollywood movie's idea of a Pole, he is not the CIA's idea of a Pole, he is not a Frenchman's idea of a Pole. He is a Pole. For ever. That aside, Bogdan's father-in-law had made it possible for him to own his own taxi in Warsaw. I am more comfortable as a cab driver, said Bogdan through Edek. Cab drivers are outside history and so they live through it. Lescek knows this and forgives me for it, Bogdan boasted. Lescek would like a quiet life too, but there is a Polish demon in him.

Halinka's talon grabbed Clancy's wrist. "They're talking just like they did in the thirties," whispered Halinka, the sound seeming to come from her stark eyes. "Demons aren't enough for them. They have to be *Polish* demons. They are awful people. Why did I come, Mr Clancy?"

Clancy thought it best to pat the stick-like wrist behind Halinka's claw. Besides, through Bogdan, he was one flight of stairs up from what every Australian desired – History; the centre.

A darkness had fallen. Street lights pocked but did not dispel it. Suddenly Edek screamed, "The Vistula! The Vistula!"

"River of such tears," murmured Halinka, lighting another cigarette.

J. M. COETZEE

J. M. COETZEE

J. M. Coetzee was born in Cape Town in 1940 and educated in South Africa and the USA, where he gained his Ph.D. from the University of Texas. Trained originally as a computer scientist and linguist, he has since 1984 been Professor of General Literature at the University of Cape Town. His publications include the novels *Dusklands* (1974), *In the Heart of the Country* (1977), *Waiting for the Barbarians* (1980), and *Foe* (1986), as well as *White Writing* (1988), a collection of criticism. As well as winning the Booker Prize for *Life & Times of Michael K* in 1983, he has won the CNA Prize (three times), the Geoffrey Faber Memorial Prize, the James Tait Black Memorial Prize, the Jerusalem Prize, and the Prix Femina Etranger.

*L*ife & Times of Michael K is a novel of extended static moments rather than of purposeful forward action. Michael's retreat into the mountains in search of independence is one of these moments, in which I tried to give simple experience its lyrical due.

Extract from *Life & Times of Michael K*

High above the town he cast around for a place to sleep and found a cave that had evidently been used before by campers. There was a stone fireplace, and a bed of fragrant dry thymebush was spread over the floor. He made a fire and roasted a lizard he had killed with a stone. The funnel of the sky above turned a darker blue and stars emerged. He curled up, tucked his hands into his sleeves, and drifted towards sleep. Already it was hard to believe that he had known someone called the Visagie grandson who had tried to turn him into a body-servant. In a day or two, he told himself, he would forget the boy and remember only the farm.

He thought of the pumpkin leaves pushing through the earth. Tomorrow will be their last day, he thought: the day after that they will wilt, and the day after that they will die, while I am out here in the mountains. Perhaps if I started at sunrise and ran all day I would not be too late to save them, them and the other seeds that are going to die underground, though they do not know it, that are never going to see the light of day. There was a cord of tenderness that stretched from him to the patch of earth beside the dam and must be cut. It seemed to him that one could cut a cord like that only so many times before it would not grow again.

He spent a day in idleness, sitting in the mouth of his cave gazing up at the farther peaks on which there were still patches of snow. He felt hungry but did nothing about it. Instead of listening to the crying of his body he tried to listen to the great silence about him. He went to sleep easily and had a dream in which he was running as fast as the wind along an open road with the cart floating behind him on tyres that barely skimmed the ground.

The sides of the valley were so steep that the sun did not emerge till noon and had gone behind the western peaks by mid afternoon. He was cold all the time. So he climbed higher, zigzagging up the slope till the road through the pass disappeared from sight and he was looking over the vast plain of the Karoo, with Prince Albert itself miles below. He found a new cave and cut bushes for the floor. He thought: Now surely I have come as far as a man can come; surely no one will be mad enough to cross these plains, climb these mountains, search these rocks to find me; surely now that in all the world only I know where I am, I can think of myself as lost.

Everything else was behind him. When he awoke in the morning he faced only the single huge block of the day, one day at a time. He thought of himself as a termite boring its way through a rock. There seemed nothing to do but live. He sat so still that it would not have startled him if birds had flown down and perched on his shoulders.

Straining his eyes he could sometimes make out the dot of a vehicle crawling down the main street of the toy town on the plain below; but even on the stillest of days no sound reached him save the scurrying of insects across the ground, and the buzz of the flies that had not forgotten him, and the pulse of blood in his ears.

He did not know what was going to happen. The story of his life had never been an interesting one; there had usually been someone to tell him what to do next; now there was no one, and the best thing seemed to be to wait.

His thoughts went to Wynberg Park, one of the places where he had worked in the old days. He remembered the young mothers who had brought their children to play on the swings and the couples lying together in the shade of the trees and the green and brown mallards in the pond. Presumably the grass had not stopped growing in Wynberg Park because there was a war, and the leaves had not stopped falling. There would always be a need for people to mow the grass and sweep up the leaves. But he was no longer sure that he would choose green lawns and oak trees to live among. When he thought of Wynberg Park he thought of an earth more vegetal than mineral, composed of last year's rotted leaves and the year before's and so on back till the beginning of time, an earth so soft that one could dig and never come to the end of the softness; one could dig to the centre of the earth from Wynberg Park, and all the way to the centre it would be cool and dark and damp and soft. I have lost my love for that kind of earth, he thought, I no longer care to feel that kind of earth between my fingers. It is no longer the green and the brown that I want but the yellow and the red; not the wet but the dry; not the dark but the light; not the soft but the hard. I am becoming a different kind of man, he thought, if there are two kinds of man. If I were cut, he thought, holding his wrists out, looking at his wrists, the blood would no longer gush from me but seep, and after a little seeping dry and heal. I am becoming smaller and harder and drier every day. If I were to die here, sitting in the mouth of my cave looking out over the plain with my knees under my chin, I would be dried out by the wind in a day, I would be preserved whole, like someone in the desert drowned in sand.

In his first days in the mountains he went for walks, turned over stones, nibbled at roots and bulbs. Once he broke open an ant nest and ate grubs one by one. They tasted like fish. But now he ceased to make an adventure of eating and drinking. He did not explore his new world. He did not turn his cave into a home or keep a record of the passage of the days. There was nothing to look forward to but the sight, every morning, of the shadow of the rim of the mountain chasing faster and faster toward him till all of a sudden he was bathed in sunlight. He would sit or lie in a stupor at the mouth of the cave, too tired to move or perhaps too lackadaisical. There were whole afternoons he slept through. He wondered if he were living in what was known as bliss. There was a day of dark cloud and rain, after which tiny pink flowers sprang up all over the mountainside, flowers without any leaf that he could see. He ate handfuls of flowers and his stomach hurt. As the days became hotter the streams ran faster, he could not see why. In this crisp mountain water he missed the bitter savour of water from under the earth. His gums bled; he drank the blood.

As a child K had been hungry, like all the children of Huis Norenius. Hunger had turned them into animals who stole from each other's plates and climbed the kitchen enclosure to rifle the garbage cans for bones and peelings. Then he had grown older and stopped wanting. Whatever the nature of the beast that had howled inside him, it was starved into stillness. His last years at Huis Norenius were the best, when there were no big boys to torment him, when he could slip off to his place behind the shed and be left alone. One of the teachers used to make his class sit with their hands on their heads, their lips pressed tightly together and their eyes closed, while he patrolled the rows with his long ruler. In time, to K, the posture grew to lose its meaning as punishment and became an avenue of reverie; he remembered sitting hands on head through hot afternoons with doves cooing in the gum trees and the chant of the tables coming from other classrooms, struggling with a delicious drowsiness. Now, in front of his cave, he sometimes locked his fingers behind his head, closed his eyes, and emptied his mind, wanting nothing, looking forward to nothing.

There were other times when his mind would return to the Visagie boy in his hiding place, wherever that was, in darkness under the floor among the mouse-droppings, or shut up in a cupboard in the attic, or out in his grandfather's veld behind a bush. He thought of the nice pair of boots: they seemed wasted on someone who lived in a hole.

It became an effort not to shut his eyes against the glare of the sun. There was a throbbing that would not leave him; lances of light pierced his head. Then he could keep nothing down; even water made him retch. There was a day when he was too tired to get up from his bed in the cave; the black coat lost its warmth and he shivered continually. It came home to him that he might die, he or his body, it was the same thing, that he might lie here till the moss on the roof grew dark before his eyes, that his story might end with his bones growing white in this far off place.

It took him all of a day to creep down the mountainside. His legs were weak, his head hammered, every time he looked downward he grew dizzy and had to grip the earth till the whirling stopped. When he reached the level of the road the valley was in deep shadow; the last light was fading by the time he entered the town. The smell of peach blossom enveloped him. There was a voice too, coming from all sides, the calm even voice he had heard the first day he saw Prince Albert. He stood at the head of the High Street among the verdant gardens unable to make out a word, though he listened hard, of the distant monotone that after a while blended with the twitter of the birds in the trees and then gave way to music.

There was no one on the streets. K made his bed in the doorway of the Volkskas office with a rubber doormat under his head. When his body had cooled he began to shiver. He slept in fits, clenching his jaws against the pain in his head. A flashlight woke him but he could not separate it from the dream in which he was involved. To the questions of the police he gave unclear answers, shouts and gasps. "Don't! . . . Don't! . . . Don't! . . ." he said, the word coming out like a cough from his lungs. Understanding nothing, repelled by his smell, they pushed him into their van, took him back to the station, and locked him in a cell with five other men, where he resumed his shivering and his delirious sleep.

In the morning, when they led the prisoners out for ablutions and breakfast, K was rational but unable to stand. He apologised to the constable at the door. "It is cramp in my legs, it will go away," he said. The constable called the duty officer. For a while they watched the skeletal figure that sat with its back to the wall rubbing its exposed calves; then together they bore K bodily into the yard, where he cringed from the brilliant sunlight, and motioned another of the prisoners to give him food. K accepted a thick slab of mealie-porridge but, even before the first spoonful had reached his mouth, had begun his retching.

No one knew where he was from. He had no papers on him, not even a green card. On the charge sheet he was listed "Michael Visagie – CM – 40 NFA – Unemployed", and charged with leaving his magisterial district without authorisation, not being in possession of an identification document, infringing the curfew, and being drunk and disorderly. Attributing his debilitation and incoherence to alcohol poisoning, they permitted him to stay in the yard while the other prisoners were returned to the cells, then at noon took him in the back of the van to the hospital. There he was stripped of his clothes and lay naked on a rubber sheet while a young nurse washed and shaved him and dressed him in a white smock. He felt no shame. "Tell me, I have always wanted to know, who is Prince Albert?" he asked the nurse. She paid no attention. "And who is Prince Alfred? Isn't there a Prince Alfred too?" He waited for the soft warm rag to touch his face, closing his eyes, willing it to come.

So he lay again between clean sheets, not in the main ward but in a long wood and iron extension at the rear of the hospital, housing, as far as he could see, only children and old men. A row of light bulbs hung on long cords from the bare rafters swaying out of time with one another. A tube ran out of his arm to a bottle on a rack; out of the corner of his eye he could watch the level fall hour by hour, if he wanted to.

Once when he awoke there were a nurse and a policeman in the doorway looking in his direction, murmuring together. The policeman carried his cap under his arm.

The afternoon sun glared through the window. A fly settled on his mouth. He waved it away. It circled and settled again. He yielded; his lip underwent the tiny cold searching of its proboscis.

An orderly came in with a trolley. Everyone got a tray except K. Smelling the food, he felt the saliva seep in his mouth. It was the first hunger he had known for a long time. He was not sure that he wanted to become a servant to hunger again; but a hospital, it seemed, was a place for bodies, where bodies asserted their rights.

Dusk fell, and then darkness. Someone switched on the lights, in two banks of three. K closed his eyes and slept. When he opened them again the lights were still on. Then as he watched they faded and went off. Moonlight fell in four silver slabs through the four windows. Somewhere nearby a diesel motor sputtered. The lights came on dimly. He fell asleep.

In the morning he ate and kept down a breakfast of baby cereal and milk. He felt strong enough to get up, but was too shy to do so till he saw an old man wrap a dressing gown over his pyjamas and leave the room. After that he walked up and down beside his bed for a while, feeling odd in the long smock.

In the next bed was a young boy with a bandaged stump of an arm. "What happened?" said K. The boy turned away and did not reply.

If I could find my clothes, K thought, I would leave. But the cupboard beside his bed was empty.

He ate again at midday. "Eat while you can," said the orderly who brought his food, "the great hunger is still to come." Then he moved on, pushing the trolley of food before him. It seemed a strange thing to say. K kept an eye on him as he went his round. From the far end of the ward the orderly felt K's gaze, and gave him a mysterious smile; but when he returned to fetch the tray he would say nothing more.

The sun beating down on the iron roof turned the ward into an oven. K lay with his legs spread, dozing. From one of his spells he awoke to see the same policeman and nurse standing over him. He shut his eyes; when he opened them they were gone. Night fell.

In the morning a nurse fetched him and led him to a bench in the main building, where he waited an hour till it was his turn. "How are you feeling today?" asked the doctor. K hesitated, not knowing what to say, and the doctor stopped listening. He told K to breathe and listened to his chest. He examined him for venereal infection. In two minutes it was over. He wrote something in the brown folder on his desk. "Have you ever seen a doctor about your mouth?" he asked while he wrote. "No," said K. "You could get it corrected, you know," said the doctor, but did not offer to correct it.

ANITA BROOKNER

ANITA BROOKNER

Anita Brookner was born in 1928 and educated at James Allen's Girls' School and King's College, University of London. She is an international authority on eighteenth- and nineteenth-century painting and has written books on Watteau, Greuze and Jacques-Louis David. She was a lecturer at the Courtauld Institute of Art and, in 1968, Slade Professor at Cambridge. *Hotel du Lac*, Anita Brookner's fourth novel, which won the Booker Prize in 1984, was preceded by *A Start in Life, Providence* and *Look at Me,* and followed by *Family and Friends, A Misalliance, A Friend from England* and *Latecomers*.

*F*amily and Friends was the novel I most enjoyed writing and I think it is my best. It came very easily, without any of the sense of strain that usually accompanies this sort of work, which is the mental equivalent of hard manual labour. I once likened writing a novel to trying very hard to remember something that has not yet happened: for me it is like dreaming while fully conscious – a dangerous state. Yet the writing of *Family and Friends* proved to me that everything is retrievable, no matter how brief its appearance in one's life. I know Nice quite well, Bordighera only slightly; both were vividly present to me when I was writing this chapter. And Frederick, the insouciant remittance man, is so delighted with his life that it was a pleasure to write about him. I remember the sun shining strongly on my back while I was engaged on this particular chapter. It was an altogether happy experience.

Extract from *Family and Friends*

Frederick, becalmed in Bordighera, rarely thinks of home. The war, which isolated them all in this little town, seems to have cut them off definitively from their roots. The war, of course, was bad for business, but for Frederick and Evie it was a time of astonishing calm, even happiness. Both have proved themselves to be fearless and adaptable in the business of survival. As soon as they saw signs of invading patrols of any description they hastened down to the enormous cellar, the existence of which very few suspected, and emerged with several choice bottles in which they insisted on drinking their visitors' health. For this reason they were soon on friendly terms with officers of more than one nationality, for the wine was too good to bring to the notice of the common soldiery who would in any case merely have smashed the bottles. With fine vintages as their currency, Evie and Frederick obtained enough food to live on and were content with simple fare – sardines and cheese and olives and bread and fruit – which kept them healthy and bright-eyed in appearance. So welcoming were Evie and Frederick, with the hoteliers' knack of instant appreciation of the client's needs, that the officers would take to dropping in to the deserted hotel in the evenings for a bottle of wine and a little relaxation; parcels of comestibles would change hands, and, after a brief wordless nod from Evie, Frederick would then proffer the fine cigars which he had saved from his father's belongings. Although war and depredation may have raged up and down the coast, all was peace and amity at the Hotel Windsor in Bordighera.

With so little to do and no guests to provide for, Evie and Frederick could concentrate more easily on each other. This war, which separated so many couples, merely reinforced their dependence on each other. It was with deep joy that they awaited the birth of their twins, attended only by the ancient village doctor, who delivered them in one of the spare rooms of the Hotel Windsor. Evie, up and about within five days, gave proof that the earthiness that had first enslaved Frederick was in fact true currency: fecund and beaming, Evie found motherhood the easiest thing in the world. Slopping around in old sandals, her springy hair slipping from its moorings, she gave evidence of a profound sluttishness; Frederick remembers her face shining moistly, her spotless tongue slipping between her unpainted lips, her effortless and unselfconscious squatting as she cleaned up a little spilt milk or one of the dog's accidents. In fact, Evie found this wartime *déshabillé* so much to her liking that, once the bad times are past, and the hotel begins to fill up again, Frederick has some difficulty in persuading her to go to the hairdresser and the dressmaker and to put on stockings and lipstick. He will always think of the essential Evie as bare legged, her feet in broken *savates*, her nightgown slightly soiled with milk, yawning and stretching in the early morning, and, half asleep, going through to the dressing-room to feed the babies. Frederick, with the finely attuned senses of a man who has always loved women, finds this scene ravishing, voluptuous. Evie, who never really worried, knows that she will not lose him now.

Frederick's earlier friends would be a little surprised to see him these days. He has put on quite a bit of weight, and his hair, now sleek and much longer, is peppered with grey. He wears cream linen trousers, a white cotton shirt, and a panama hat. Only the pale narrow shoes reveal the cad and the dandy that Frederick used to be. This uniform is unvarying. The hat is in place when Frederick enters the hotel lounge from his private quarters at nine o'clock every morning. He has already been to the station for the newspapers, which he places on the glass-topped wicker tables, and then he briefly takes a turn in the garden, where the gardener's hosepipe is playing on the tubs of orange trees. After this he is more or less free until the evening, for Evie has wisely decided to treat him as if he were a boy, on holiday from school, which is exactly how Frederick feels. It is this odd mixture of juvenility and paunchy assiduity that would confound Frederick's earlier friends. In his panama hat and his pale shoes, his short-sleeved shirt, in the breast pocket of which his lunchtime cigar is visible, and the slightly fatuous smile of contentment on his face, Frederick seems as disarmed and as disarming as any innocent tourist. Frederick has always been a tourist rather than a traveller. He has no real interest in one place as against any other. He appears to see no differences in landscape or customs provided that his own comforts are assured and his habits safely accommodated. He accepts the Hotel Windsor as his home in much the same way that he once took his ease in his mother's house. A faintly patronal air was there from the start, and, by the same token, the good manners of the excellent guest that he always was. Frederick was the guest of his mother; rising from his chair in her drawing room to welcome the friends who used to come for coffee and marzipan cake on a Sunday afternoon, he would have the same expansive and attentive air that he now uses to such good purpose in his new trade. What would puzzle his friends, apart from Frederick's appearance, would be to see this process reversed, to see assiduity shading into automatic *bonhomie*, and the patron only taking his ease when the demands of the guests have been attended to.

Yet Frederick has no idea that a shift has taken place in both his fortunes and his reputation. This may be, of course, because there is no one around from the old days to witness the change. Is it perhaps for this reason that Frederick feels an instinctive reluctance towards the mere idea of going home for a visit? Does he know that this combination, so marvellously to his taste, of Evie's sluttishness and his own dandyish but decidedly foreign appearance, might not pass muster with his mother, his brother, under the weeping skies of London, a city which now appears to him as small, huddled, grey, and unheroic? By unheroic Frederick implies no moral failing; morals rarely come into his equations. In any event he has had no need of heroism himself; the cellars have furnished him with an easier means of exchange. No, by unheroic Frederick understands himself to mean dreary, lacking in expansion, lacking in physical excellence. Frederick, acute always to the implications of colour, outline, the elegance of silhouette, the charm of appearance, far prefers this little town, where, under skies as blue and as cloudless as the inside of a painted cup, he can stroll down the Corso Italia and see nothing less harmonious than the jagged leaves of an overgrown palm tree. Stepping delicately but briskly down the Corso on his way to the station, Frederick will see oranges and lemons growing on trees; he will see and smell the café with its gusts of vanilla and its squawking coffee machines; he will greet the spotless and handsome waiter opening up the restaurant for an airing before lunch; and he will wave to the old lady who keeps the ironmonger's and for whom he will sometimes take a letter to the post. In this way, the golden light that illuminates Frederick's early morning excursion will have effectively blotted out the sparse colour and harsh winds of London, where he feels he would no longer be at home. In any case, he knows that the old house has been sold and that the family has moved to Bryanston Square; it would hardly count as going home now even if he were to go back. Frederick feels that the family has moved away from him rather than the other way around. In any event, under the impact of this unvarying light, it is very difficult to imagine himself returning to anything less brilliant, less natural, less effortless than this place. Frederick, like any other instinctive creature, espouses a habitat where he is most at ease.

Of course, he will go home some day and see his mother; he has promised her as much. And of course she must see her grandchildren, his children, of whom he is immensely proud. In a way it would have been a good idea to go back for Mimi's wedding, the news of which came as a considerable surprise. But after happy days in his pale shoes and his panama hat Frederick cannot quite see himself in the solemnity of a morning coat and in a crush of relations. He really does not care for all those people any more: his mother and his sister he prefers to cherish as golden presences about his early youth, unmarked by age or care or change. He thinks it not a bad idea that Mimi should marry Lautner. They both, he sees, have some quality of gravity which makes them natural partners but with which he was never completely at ease. And he likes to think of an additional member of staff, as it were, on duty to care for his mother. In a way, it is as if Lautner were substituting for himself as he so often did in the past. Yes, he is all for the marriage, but as he sees it there is no longer any reason for him to be present. If Lautner is there then Frederick is relieved of his duties. He sends a telegram, of course, and treats himself to a cognac after lunch in which he drinks his sister's health.

Frederick's contacts with England are now confined to whatever Sofka and Mimi care to send. A constant stream of requests for Start-Rite shoes, Dundee marmalade, and Floris's New Mown Hay goes out from Bordighera to London and is answered by carefully packed parcels and letters of credit to a bank in Nice. Alfred has proved remarkably successful in business, as Frederick always knew that he would, and Frederick has no qualms in asking for some of the profits, for which, as he sees it, he is partly responsible. Besides, the hotel needs extra staff and the money has to come from somewhere; Evie's Dadda lost quite a bit in the war, and she feels that he deserves great sympathy in this respect; the funds in Switzerland are not to be drawn on until Dadda dies, and anyway that money will come to Evie. It is only right that this money should be balanced by something from the other side of the family. In this way Frederick manages to think of England as a place of funds and commodities, devoted to that business which he always disliked, and functioning as a service area for places of natural enchantment and superiority where lives may be more pleasantly and more attractively lived. If there is any hint of filial impiety from Alfred, whose letters are curt and without affection, Frederick has one unanswerable trump card: he has fathered twins. He is, of all Sofka's children, the only one who has gone forth and multiplied. There can be no criticism that will not be nullified by this evidence of fruitfulness. By this very act of fathering his children Frederick has placed himself beyond reproach.

And he loves those children, who so resemble their mother, and who, in response to their mother's excellent nurturing instinct, grew up without problems, without those little finicky appetites which had always dogged his brother and his sisters, without faces pale and temples hollowed by the hours of reading that he remembers as such a feature of his own youth. Frederick's children, Erica and Thomas, have always slept through the night and have eaten everything that is given to them. They enjoy scratched legs, dirty faces, and days in the open air; they flourish on the intermittent hygiene meted out by their mother, on the inappropriate menus which come down to them from the hotel dining room, and from the ice-creams at the café for which Frederick always slips them money. Erica and Thomas speak Italian and a sort of French, both with lingering uneducated accents; they are sharp and resourceful children, and they will never be properly educated. In many ways they resemble the children of the environs; canny and quick and very slightly underhand. They will do well, and they will never go home. Yet, with their square teeth and their Start-Rite shoes, they grin convincingly enough in the photographs which Frederick sends home to his mother to set her murmuring about resemblances and peering at the tiny faces in an effort to see reflected there the image of her beloved son.

On this sunny morning, as on so many others, Frederick walks down the Corso Italia, turning his head from side to side the better to savour the varied delights that are brought to the attention of his senses: the smell of vanilla from the café, the hose playing about the orange-tree tubs in the garden, the pleasant bustle of early morning, and the impeccable sky of uninflected blue. Despite the charms of Bordighera, Frederick is making for Nice, as is his habit. If the car is not free he will take the train, which saves him a lot of trouble at the frontier even if it does take a little longer. He is usually in Nice by midday and he takes a taxi to the old town so that he can spend an hour in the market before sitting down to a pleasant lunch in any of half a dozen favourite places behind the harbour. Frederick will rarely buy anything in the market but the place has become essential to him as a storehouse of further sights, smells, and impressions to feed his ever greedy sensorium. From the flower market, with its tightly-furled bouquets of carnations – red, pink, white, yellow, striped, and even dyed blue – Frederick will penetrate to the inner secret depths of the old town. Here, on precipitously stepped and cobbled streets, twisting blindly and abruptly around corners and slippery with fish scales, Frederick will tread carefully in his pale shoes, tipping his hat to those stall holders who recognise him from previous visits. He will appreciate, with an equal and a discerning eye, a tuft of coarse grass thrusting up through the cobbles where the alley meets the wall of the church of St Rita, the butcher's boy emerging with uplifted hatchet from the back of the shop to check on the symmetry and the quantity of the day's display of lamb chops in white enamelled trays, the priest with his long soutane and his furled black hat, the basket of cheap but elegant shoes in the doorway of a shop so dark that it is necessary to put most of its goods on the pavement, the sharp and almost sickening smell of the cheeses laid out on leaves of fern and palm, the sudden gleam of a coffee machine and the spurt of its steam, the blessed sight of the fresh loaves of bread, newly baked for lunchtime, being set up vertically in the window of the baker's shop. Sometimes Frederick will imagine himself loading baskets with sticks of bread, and portions of different paté – the rabbit, the goose, the hare – and bushels of mirabelle plums, and taking those baskets somewhere where he and Evie can steal away from the children and eat. But as he is on his own, Frederick puts his excellent sensual imagination to work and enjoys, vicariously, the delights which the shopkeepers and stall holders arrange for his delectation. Frederick is such a happy man, so elegant, so smiling, as he wends his way down the slippery and sharply-descending streets, that everyone gives him a greeting; it hardly matters that he never buys anything, for he has become in a sense the spirit of the place, if not its patron, and merely to see him there in his pale shoes and his immaculate shirt and his panama hat is to receive a lift to the heart, as if this market, in which humbler people ply their trades, has been granted a certificate of excellence from the most enlightened of connoisseurs. Frederick raises his hat to old ladies in black who have slipped out for a cutlet and a bottle of wine and a *baguette* for their lunch; he notices the sinewy cats that weave figures of eight around the old ladies' slippered feet, and he empathetically imagines that he too is an old lady, free at last to please herself, to get fat, and let her feet go, and emerge from aromatic gloom to the dark blue sky above and the dusky smell of the cheese shop and the cool shape of the bottle in one's hand and the prospect of a long siesta. Frederick raises his hat to the priest, and, for courtesy's sake, enters the small hot gaudy church of St Rita and slips some money into the wooden box; sometimes he lights a tapering candle, for the sheer pleasure of seeing the flame reluctantly take hold and climb up the white unsullied wick and achieve a steady pale glow; he will sniff the incense with the same careful nose that he once laid to a cigar. Finally, he will take a small cup of black coffee standing at the counter of a dark café, a mere tunnel between two shops, glittering with the chrome of its coffee machine and alive with the cries and greeting of the midday clientele. Here, too, he is known.

"*Eh bien, M'sieu Frédéric, ça va, la santé.*"

"*Très bien, Martial, je vous remercie.*"

"*Qu'est-ce qu'on vous sert aujourd'hui, M'sieu Frédéric?*"

"*Un express et un verre d'eau fraîche, s'il vous plaît, Martial.*"

For Frederick rarely drinks, and in any case seems to despise any additional stimulus which might heighten and ultimately falsify his own excellent imagination.

Finally, as the crowd drifts away from the café, Frederick takes his leave of the owner, settles his hat once more on his head, and goes out in search of lunch. He prefers to leave it late, for then he can enjoy the spectacle of the Vieux Port slumbering in the early afternoon heat as he sips his coffee and lights his cigar on the terrace of whatever restaurant he has chosen for that day. Frederick is abstemious, and although no longer mindful of his thickening waistline, prefers to eat a modest meal, perhaps merely a grilled sole or an escalope of veal and a little *salade cuite*, before settling down to his half hour of contemplation with his coffee and his cigar. Now the sky is powdery white with heat and he can no longer make out the horizon; cars dazzle him with the reflection of the sun on their chrome, and in the longer and longer intervals of quiet, he can hear the creaking of the masts of the little boats in the harbour. Draining his coffee cup, Frederick asks for the bill, enquires after the health of the lady at the cash desk who nods to him and mimics a reply, and glances to left and right before deciding which route to take to his afternoon place of entertainment. He will either walk along the front, made giddy by the brilliant light and the swoop of traffic, or, more usually, thread his way through the back streets, where trees and rough pavements soon give way to commercial arcades selling the sort of odourless and manufactured produce for which Frederick has no use: magazines, sun glasses, picture postcards, stamps. Once past the Place Masséna, the town is of no further interest to him. He hardly notices it.

At the Ruhl they know him, of course. They are assured that he will spend no more than an hour at the tables, that he will bet modestly, and neither win nor lose a great deal, and that he will be on respectful and easy terms with the ladies who come there, carefully coiffed and made-up, every afternoon, ostensibly to take tea, in fact to attach to themselves a dancing partner, even if they have to pay for one. Frederick is at ease here, and the management are always pleased to see him; his good nature and his good manners ensure that no lady will remain too pathetically and too obviously on her own for more than five or ten minutes. Compliments have always come easily to Frederick; therefore he considers it quite natural to steer these ladies round the tables and to offer them tea. Sometimes the ladies order something stronger and suggest that he stay on for dinner, but Frederick has never cared for that sort of behaviour. In Frederick's universe, the man offers and the woman gratifies. It would seem a reversal of the natural order to proceed in any other way, and indeed he has never needed to do so. Therefore, after a cup of lemon tea and a little expert and desultory conversation, so that the lady should not feel herself to have been offended, he looks around for his panama hat, stands up, and, kissing the lady's hand, takes his leave.

He never stays later than four o'clock. By this time he is feeling a little tired, a little less than the immaculate self which he presented to the world that morning, in the shining air of Bordighera. On the train he pats down a yawn and applies himself to the evening paper which he has bought at the station, noticing with a slight exclamation of distaste that the print has soiled his hands. No matter; at the Hotel Windsor he will ask the upstairs chambermaid Maria to draw his bath as soon as he gets back, and he will recline in the coolish water, scented with New Mown Hay, until he feels his energies return. Then he will dress in his hotelier's evening wear: an immaculate pale cotton suit with matching tie, a fresh shirt, a clean linen handkerchief. He will smooth his sleek greying hair down with his father's silver brushes, which came to him as a matter of course, and, no longer noticing his pear-shaped figure or his dark brown face, he will go downstairs, and, with a discreet but none the less heartfelt kiss, will imply to Evie that she is now free until dinner.

These early evening hours are when Frederick both lays himself out to please and excels himself. Not a guest enters the lobby of the Hotel Windsor after a weary day on the beach or sight-seeing further down the coast but does not feel a lightening of the spirit on encountering Frederick in his pale blue or his pale grey suit, always ready to order a late cup of tea for them and to hear about their day's adventures. Frederick's sybaritic leanings incline him towards indulgence and he has a special smile with which he listens to feminine chatter; it is with a lighter step that so many women guests go up to take their baths and to decide what to wear for the evening. Dinner is a fairly formal affair: Evie and Frederick dine together at a small table slightly out of earshot of the other guests; the children having eaten earlier, either in their suite, if the maids are not too busy, or, more probably, in the kitchen, where they can more easily satisfy their robust appetites. Evie and Frederick have coffee served for all in the salon rather than at the tables, an English habit which makes a favourable impression on the guests, many of whom have returned to the hotel two or three times. When they have enquired after the health of the one or two carefully selected retired couples who intend to spend the winter there, Evie and Frederick tend to say goodnight to everyone and to slip out, knowing that they have stimulated the sort of remarks which will be made about them in their absence. "A quite devoted couple, it seems." "Yes, isn't it charming? And they always take this evening walk together before they retire for the night. I find it quite touching." "So delightful. It makes for such a pleasant atmosphere."

In the scented night Evie and Frederick take their late walk, arm in arm, sometimes hand in hand. The sky is now an impenetrable indigo, yet along the horizon there is still a faint smudge of salmon-coloured brilliance. The wind rustles the leathery palm leaves and the oranges and lemons glow on the trees as if lit from within. Amber light gushes from the café, where the coffee machine gleams and the scent of vanilla is now mingled with the aroma of cigarettes. Evie and Frederick walk up the steep Corso Italia, away from the sea, away from the station, to the higher ground above the little town. Here, like an elderly couple, they sit on a municipal seat, and here Frederick smokes his second and last cigar of the day. They sit in wordless companionship, looking down on the dark vulture-like shapes of the palm trees, hearing nothing but the whine of a passing moped. Strange, how peaceable Evie has become, she who used to be so noisy and so disruptive. Strange, how excellent this marriage has proved to be, the man offering, the woman gratifying. Strange, how fearless and how original they are away from the constrictions of home and family. Strange, how rooted they appear to be in this frivolous place, divorced from serious need or concern. Soon they will rise to their feet, take each other's hand, and slowly wander back to the Hotel Windsor. They will appreciate the new keenness of the air as a little wind blows up and the houses darken. In their room they will find the bed turned down on both sides, and the shutters closed. Evie will light an incense stick to keep mosquitoes at bay. In no more than a few minutes they will have undressed, kissed, and fallen asleep, safe and calm in the conviction of another beautiful day tomorrow, under the same unalterable sky.

No wonder Frederick never seriously considers going home again.

KERI HULME

KERI HULME

Of Maori, Scots and English ancestry, the author was born in Christchurch and now makes her home on the West Coast of New Zealand – in a house she built herself.

In the past, she has worked at many jobs, ranging from tobacco picker to pharmacist's assistant, but now she is a full time writer, painter and whitebaiter. Her poems and short stories have been published in many magazines and broadcast on radio and television; *The Silences Between: Moeraki Conversations* – a book of poetry and prose – was published in 1982 by Auckland University Press and *The Bone People*, first published in 1984 by the Spiral Collective, won the Pegasus Prize for Maori Literature as well as the Booker Prize in 1985.

Floating Words

THINKING BACK
(I am balanced on the end bollard, the slip-rope in my hand)
there were omens all along.

For example, quite early on, before anything began to move, a kingfisher perched on the powerlines, a sprat in its bill. Kingfishers quite often perch on powerlines, but this one stayed there all day. The sprat kept twitching – at least, every time I looked out and saw the kingfisher still there, the sprat would spasm again. All of us who were here, then, noticed the bird and the fish, and we all commented on it, but none of us wondered about it in depth. None of us saw the kingfisher fly away, either. Presumably the sprat was eventually swallowed.

THERE WAS ALSO the last time I picked mushrooms.

It had been drizzling for days. Normally the mid-year is rain-time, two or three inches a day, a night, but the weather turned lazy. Endless days masked in misty feeble drizzle. So I had put off going out for mushrooms, and put off and put off until one day my hunger for them overcame my sense. Our mushroom fields are – were – different. It's all agaricales here, bitorquis and subperonatus mainly, but occasionally a broad fat arvensis, eagerly sought for because of its rich taste. They grow along the airstrip, half a mile of sheep-shorn grass, and throughout the picnic areas. Even then, the sea edging in from the south had whittled the picnic areas away, and the remaining knobs of sheep dung on the strip had a sad grey patina to them. The sheep themselves had been trucked away, weeks before.

I amble along the strip, seemingly aimlessly. When I first went gathering, I would mistake driftwood and pallid stones and old gnawed bits of sheepbone for mushrooms, because I made the mistake of *looking* for them. That was years ago; now I have my eye in. Now I wander, humming quietly. There is a rusty brown cap, barely thumbnail-sized; there is a handwide parasol; here is a clutch of beauties, their tops pale as eggs. I have nearly a bag full when I stop midway down the strip.

There is a thick white mist, north, and I can no longer see Abut Head. The mail-blimp said it has retreated, two miles or more she said. The Tasman runs fierce and wild just over a new stonebank; it has come in another chain since I was here last.

I sigh: Change, change, change. Where is solidity? Where is the rock?

Turning south again to finish gathering from the strip, my eye is caught by something odd-looking, wrong, out-of-place. A burst of colour by a clump of toetoe. It looks, upon examination, like a bolete – well, it has that family's spongy tissue under the cap – but it is coloured like no bolete I have ever heard of. There is a repulsive fungus from Haast called Tylopilus formosus, which is brown-black on top, and a horrid livid pink undercap; there is a variety of hygrophorus named 'multicolour' which is red and green and sulphur yellow *outside*, and turquoise blue *inside*. This thing looks like a mismatch between them. Greeny black on top, and blue underneath, and red and yellow in alternate bands up the length of the stalk.

No way am I going to eat it, but I want to know more about it, so I disengage it from the sand with care, and weave a swift rough kete from toetoe leaves to bear it home. And bear it home on bleeding fingers I do: not for nothing is toetoe known as cutty-grass.

In the misty distance is a shy retreating figure, a grey shadow in the drizzle. Though there are so few of us left, it makes no move towards me. That is understandable. Mushroom-pickers are solitary creatures, and don't like other mushroom pickers too close.

I REMEMBER THAT the mushroom caps were slightly slimy from the continuous drizzle, and that there was more sand than usual in the gills. Cooking them: half a cup of extra virgin olive oil, salt, two crushed cloves of garlic, and a lot of shredded parsley (my herbs transferred surprisingly well to buckets and terracotta pots upstairs) . . . add the mushrooms, and let all stew. A relishsome mix, that would be perfect with bacon chunks.

There hasn't been bacon available – or any meat – for months.

THERE WERE NO abnormal dreams that I recall. Flood dreams, yes: but everybody had those, conjured by the news reports (while transmission lasted).

I feel there should have been intimations of what was going on, shadows and forebodings. To the contrary: my dreams were peaceful and curiously green/rustic/waterless.

THEN THERE WAS the visitor.

Now, she was a sign of the times to come if ever there was one.

It was quite early on, after the water began rising, before the bubble cities came. I'd been writing hard, because the mail-blimp system was well-established and dependable. I never did find out who started it, how credit was established, but it worked:

"I need

*flour (stone-ground, organically-grown, from Kaikoura)

*cheese (Hipi-ma, please)

*oil (olive, and avocado)

*shoyu

*cider vinegar (Healtheries) and

*dried apricots (any left from Roxburgh?)

Herewith chapter 23."

And the mail-blimp received note and chapter, and handed over last week's order (Motueka tobacco, and NiuGinea blue-mountain beans, and a crate of Havill's Mazer Mead). The more detailed the order, the better your chances of getting anything. For some reason, never divulged, you would only receive processed food or drink. No fresh fruit or vegetables: no meat (not even salami). And if no writing accompanied the order, all that came back was a small recycled-cardboard box, with an exclamation mark made of paua-shell inside. Someone out there had a sense of humour. I only tried to gain credit without payment of words, once . . .

Anyway, I had been writing hard, all that day, most of the evening. After twenty hours at it, I was as March roes on a flounder, blackened, emptied, sour. In a mood only for a bottle of mead, and then to bed and oblivion. I'd finished 47, and got this far on the opening of the tangihanga chapter (not the end one, as you might think, but the beginning of the second section):

The coffin was really starting to brew.
The strong midday sun, of course, and the fact that they hadn't found him before the river had kept him for a week: the morgue people had done their best but it clearly wasn't enough to offset the work of the eels and the water, and it wasn't going to be sufficient to keep him together for the whole three days.

Good enough for starters, I thought, and then there's a knock on the door.
– Who is it?
Silence.
– Who *is* it?
More silence. Then the knock, tat-tat-tat BAM, three times the knuckles and once the open hand, *my* knock damn it (my pulse quickening), redoubled in force.
Piss on you too, I think, but it is the fag-end of a hard day, and it would be nicer to share a bottle of mead with a guest, than drink it in moody solitude.
I check that the cutdown .410 is there, ready on the back of the door (it is) and that the waddy is waiting to one side (it is), and then I slide the dead-bolt.
She says, in a voice full of disappointment,
– You're fatter than I thought you'd be.
I stand there, gawping.
– Bit of a sag-belly too eh?
and pushes past, headed straight for my grog cabinet.
Her hand brings out the bottle of Lagavulin without hesitation, although it is cunningly hidden by a row of other, lesser, single malts, and she knows exactly where I keep my scotch glasses, in a cupboard in the desk. She even picks out my favourite one before sprawling down on the best chair.

– You still got your 'fridge in the garage? Get us a bottle of milk eh?

– Rup bup bup . . .

Well, even I'd ignore that sort of noise.

She's started singing,

> *O yeah so I bear*
> *the stigmata*
> *of the hard drinker*
> *a doer a goer*
> *a wine-cup thinker – still*
> *will you barter*
> *your dreams for*
> *mine?*

O I know that song, Wine-song #33, early one of a long-running unpublished series . . .

– Milk eh?

There is a subtle menacing emphasis on that last "eh?". It is exactly the subtle menacing emphasis I use myself when some younger member of the family group has grown tiresomely obtuse. It warns, You don't oblige/get your act together *immediately*, someone round here is going to regret what happens next.

I'd just love to see you try, woman! I outweigh you by, o I'd say a stone and a half . . . but your hands have that tough corded look mine lost years ago. And you look meaner, as well as leaner. So we won't try fisticuffs. Yet.

She's smiling a mean lean smile.

I go out and get the milk (which comes in plastic sachets, these days. Interesting, I suddenly think, remembering "still got your 'fridge in the garage?" Even in this dazed state that is sufficient to suggest time lags.) I grab my last bottle of Lindauer's finest. Ultra Brut Cuvee Sans Dosage. That's about as mean, and lean, a champagne as you'll get, anywhere.

I can already see, despite disbelief – it's like reality has sneezed, and split – it is going to be one of those occasions where sober straight forward action will get me nowhere.

The winter moon that night was very pale.

"A pale moon doth rain."

A LONG TIME AGO, when I first started coining whakatauki-waina, aphorisms that could be, or become, proverbial sayings, I had as my initial effort:

"When you are drowning, the depth of the water is of last concern."

The essential requirement of a whakatauki-waina is that it seems to make sense – it *does* make sense, a kind of sense, but that sense is edgy and changeable, and if you think too much about it, you step into mental quicksand, skiddy and sinking all at once. That's why they're *wine* proverbs, not too much use or good anywhen else.

Aue! Whakatauki-waina; my family group; the last bottle of Lindauer, and the comparatively easy task of dealing with an imaginary clone of myself turned real. It all seems so remote and innocent these days . . .

THEN, OF COURSE, I thought the world had gone mad.

There I was, drowning in unreality, and the depth of the wine the last concern.

Half a bottle gone, half a bottle to go. There she sits, sipping whisky curds, feet propped up on a stool, sharkskin boots too close to my thigh. She wears her hair plaited in a short thick club covering the back of her neck. She has seven silver rings on her fingers, and her shirt is earth-red. The kilt is new, hand-woven hodden, with no elaborate pleats, a simple drape and fold secured by a thin black belt. The kilt is different: I hadn't ever visualised the kilt.

– You're staying long? My query sounds desperate. I am desperate.

She smiles evilly, and adds more whisky to the clabber.

– What brought you here? I mean, from – there? and she just flicks out her ball lightning, the personal charge every woman in that fantasy of mine carried, flicks out a tiny part of her lightning at a passing mosquito and zapples it dead.

IT COULD HAVE BEEN disastrous: it could have been my end. After I'd got rid of Kei-Tu, I became very leary about who

I fantasised: it was one thing putting people down on paper, quite another to have them lying, vomit-covered and comatose drunk on the floor (a whole bottle of Lagavulin, even when ruined by 2 litres of milk, does that to the most hardened drinker). I remembered that shadowy person I had seen while mushroom-picking: about my height, about my size. The skittery way it moved. Could it have been the Weever, with her monochromatic tattoos and blank assassin's eyes? I shuddered. I had invented too many characters I wouldn't want to meet. When I wrote my chapters now, to earn the daily bread (polenta/straw mushrooms/lentils), I avoided detail, intensity, realism . . . it didn't seem to matter to whoever – or whatever – read them at the other end.

IT WAS ABOUT THIS TIME that my neighbour broke down her top-storey and turned it into a giant square raft, like a cattle ferry. She built a small A-frame house upon it, and left the rest of the raft to the oyster spat she imported. The oysters grew, and spawned, and grew. She poles her oyster farm from the remaining houses, to the fortified village that juts over the swamp bay, to that eerie half-submerged colony of dirt-coloured domes which appeared overnight where the wharf-shed used to be, and trades oysters for what we have to offer.

She says, only a wet-suited arm ever comes out of the dome-colony hatch. She says, they produce interesting syrups. She says, all the men have now shifted into the fortified village, and have started a long-house culture there. Even Bond. Lux Malone scowls.

Bond had been her mate.

I say quickly,

– Have you noticed other changes?

She scratches her thigh thoughtfully. She is leaning on the long manuka pole she uses to shift around her oyster farm.

– I heard they are catching blue-eyed koura up the hill.

– Do they do anything? The koura I mean? Smarter, or more dangerous?

– Nah, sweeter . . .

Her tribe of gathered-in children skitter around the oyster farm in pirogues as sharp and swift as flick-knives. Their voices are sweet and high, but their words are unintelligible. I swap her a bunch of dried thyme and a small bottle of ngaio oil for keeping the sandflies at bay, and get a sack of oysters.

– See you, Lux . . .

– Yeah, see you –

But we probably won't. Our worlds are drifting further apart.

THE TIDE HAS reached my front fence, and the porch is dancing with a thousand whirling leaves from the dying peppermint gum. Ah wind, blow the mists away . . .

I continue creosoting the bottom storey. I have put on four coats already, and the fumes make for heady working, but more is needed. Creosote is going to be the only thing that will keep the lower portion of the house from rotting as the water rises. I have shifted all the books upstairs – the rooms there stand twelve feet above what used to be the ground. I have made a sign, FREE LIBRARY, and left the seaward door unlocked.

I've also left all the gear I won't be taking out on a raft by the gate. As I wade out with another armload (two Rust pots, an early Colin McCahon, and four spare duvets), I see that the pile is diminishing. Someone takes it away, the men from the fortified village, maybe the arms from the domes. Perhaps it is just the tide.

The barge is nearly ready: I've used the boards from the erstwhile high fence round my house (I turn the fenceposts into bollards). They are treated Kanikatea, long-lasting in water and easy to work. It's a large barge, thirty-six feet long and twenty feet wide. Working slowly, steadily, I transfer my main living room onto it. I become experienced with pulleys and levers, and don't have much trouble, even with the York Seal range. Indeed, the only trouble I've had shifting things has been with the lemon bush and the Cox's Orange apple tree: they sulked when first wrenched, and stubbornly refuse to flourish now, despite being in great wicker baskets with rich soil and room for their roots to spread. Never mind: they'll get used to the fact that nothing is static, settled, or permanent any more, least of all trees.

The sea laps my outside steps, and the crabs crawl up and patter among the dead gum leaves.

THE BUBBLE HOUSES are so common these days I no

longer bother to count them. I used to sit for hours on the upstairs shadow deck, a little mechanical KouSeiki counter in hand, and click them off as they loomed out of the mist.

1187

1188

Sometimes I would see people leaning against the transparent sides. Some of them looked trapped, others relaxed tourists of the air. 1189 1190 1191

So: some of us are drifting away by water, and some by the currents of heaven.

THE MAIL BLIMP ARRIVES for the last time. The head controlling it is not the usual elderly woman's, but one I know all too well. Every day in the mirror . . .

– I thought the crabs got you, I stammer (remembering the flaccid rolling corpse, remembering the temptation to try bacon of the unsalted kind (but that seemed to go too close to the bone)).

– The crabs never got anything that counted, says Kei-Tu, and her smile promises revenge.

I take out a packet of Angus McNeil Seasmoke salmon slices, two phials of aromatic oils (Healtheries ylangylang, and venom), a quart jar of Vegemite (Sanitarium) and a sack of wild rice. I put in the last chapter of *The Neverending Novel*, and a mail redirection-order (so to speak), but I don't think the latter will work.

– Who is looking after your books? asks Kei-Tu. My library used to be famous.

– Any reader . . .

– Where are you going?

– I don't know. Wherever the inward and ingoing tides take me. To stop temporarily wherever I strand.

Storytellers never stay in one place for long.

But I have spent too many words on my reply for the mail blimp has already risen and floated away.

STANDING ON THE DECK of my home-made-boat, I stare at the strange bolete. It had not shrivelled or decayed over the months, but extended hyphae through the rough little toetoe kete, and made the whole its mycellium. That is unnatural, hyphae being delicate and exceedingly vulnerable to changes in moisture or light – but what is natural now? I have seen a nest of shining cuckoos, and tresses growing from a skull . . .

I had grown used to the basket-mycellium, grown used to the violent coloration. But now the fungus is glowing with minute blue sine waves moving up the stalk as the tide rises. It is the tide in microcosm, the whole cap becoming alight at slackwater.

I recognise a sign when I am given one so clearly.

I TAKE

the tide-bolete and the weather-clock

a blanket and a swandri and six silk shirts

a black iron kettle, a skillet and a griddle

a guitar and my favourite glass

the dictionaries – OED & Partridge for English, Williams, Treagar and Biggs for Maori, and Kraz for Chaotic: no other reference books. What I don't know now, I'll make up

sundry other things like food and drink and firing

myself

ONCE UPON A TIME, we were a community *here*, ten households of people pottering through our days. We grumbled at taxes and sometimes complained about the weather. We cheered one another through the grey times, with bonfires and whisky and brisk massages. We sometimes sang when we were sad. We knew – the television told us, the radio mentioned it often – that the oceans would rise, the greenhouse effect would change the weather, and there could be rumblings and distortions along the crustal plates as Gaia adjusted to a different pressure of water. And we understood it to be one more ordinary change in the everlasting cycle of life.

Now, *here* is wherever you find me, and nowhere is where I'll be.

I AM BALANCED on the end bollard, the slip-rope in my hand.

There is one thing left to do before I jump aboard and drift away with my sulking trees.

I can't call this thing the Hulmeship: how about *Thumb-to-Nose*? Some great name from the past – *Sojourner Truth*? *The Stephen Hawking*? *Motoitoi Kahutia*? No: they are too great for a little boat whose only real freight is words. *Fish Dreaming*: now, that is poetic but I am afraid it isn't true. I wish it was.

The mists billow as land pulls away from sea, as another rift in reality occurs: a high-voiced flock of birds loops and twists round a passing stream of bubbles.

The Pirate Epistle enters your sphere.

KINGSLEY AMIS

KINGSLEY AMIS

Kingsley Amis was born in 1922. He was educated at St John's, Oxford, of which he became an Honorary Fellow in 1976. After Army service during the war, he became a Lecturer at University College, Swansea, of which he is also an Honorary Fellow. His first novel, *Lucky Jim* (1954) brought him immediate fame which was spread even more widely when it was filmed three years later. Since then there have been sixteen novels and four books of poetry, as well as books of short stories and *belles lettres*. He won the Booker Prize in 1986 with *The Old Devils*.

The Lobster's Claw

In about 1970 a South African businessman named Harold Soref, under the apparent impression that I had some time for his country's system, tried to persuade me to write a laudatory article about it. Also involved were my old friend John Braine, evidently an acquaintance of Soref's, and some fourth party whose exact role now escapes me.

"But I don't know anything about South Africa bar what I read in the papers," I kept saying.

"Don't worry, you'll get all the information you need," said the fourth chap.

"But no one thinks of me as a South Africa expert," I said.

"That'll give it all the more weight," he said.

Soref threw the four of us a lunch at the Reform Club. I shouldn't really have gone, but I am an inveterate luncher, curiosity called as ever, and I had made it clear that I was committed to nothing but to listen. It would be churlish to say that I don't even greatly care for the Reform in particular, with its absence of a proper bar, nor for the arrangement whereby the host orders the food off the menu for the whole party, thus putting pressure on them to follow his choice (and the set meal). But what the hell.

We got our pre-lunch drink, but in conditions that made it impossible to enjoy it properly. All too soon we found ourselves at the table being ordered for. I went along with the others until plumping for something that wasn't on the set lunch, liver and bacon, I think, or duckling, something far from dear, anyway, at 7s.6d, say £3.00 at today's prices. Very ungraciously, I thought, though unsuccessfully, Soref tried to block this. Much more seriously, he was shy on the booze.

Right, my lad, I thought, it may take a year, it may take five, but you'll be getting it back for this. A lot of fiction is revenge for scores of one size or sort or another. A lot more is fantasy-revenge, so that when we get to the corresponding point in my novel, instead of me just tamely sticking to my liver and bacon, my hero, Sir Roy Vandervane, insists on the priciest dish he can think up. And of course there are all sorts of other changes too. What you put into fiction isn't the things that happen to you, it's what the things that happen to you make you think up. (I might add that a lot more fiction comes from a desire to behave more badly than one would ever dare to in real life while sort of apologising for it at the same time, as is shown in episodes in my novels from *Lucky Jim* on.)

So to the scene I actually wrote in *Girl, 20*. The Reform has of course become the Retrenchment Club, "I" have split into the famous musician, Roy Vandervane, and a journalist friend of his called Douglas "Duggers", chap number four has vanished altogether, and Soref has become a newspaper editor called Harold Meers with, it turns out later, a very nasty plot up his sleeve for Roy (nothing to do with South Africa or articles about it.)

As we see, Roy gets his way over the food and drink, but he later takes a thorough beating from Meers over the plot and only wins in the end by sheer undeserved good luck. And that's very like life: just when we think we're on top, fate is preparing something specially horrible for us. Nevertheless, take care, all you who entertain writers or who have dealings with them of any sort, and reflect that it is they who have the last word.

Extract from *Girl, 20*

We had entered a room several times the size of the house I occupied half of, opulent, classical and also strongly ecclesiastical in feeling, like an early Christian emperor's orgy chamber. Soberly dressed men in twos and threes straggled across a marble floor to a battered tin cart from which drinks were unhurriedly being dispensed. Roy led the way to the rear of this queue.

"Hadn't we better inquire for him?" I asked.

"Bugger that. This was his idea. Let him find us."

He did when we were about halfway to the drinks cart. First he and Roy, then he and I, nodded at each other. Harold's second nod led without a break into a glance at his watch.

"Time's getting on," he said. "This confounded insistence on ice in everything. A lot of stuff piled up. Do you mind if we have a drink at the table?"

"No, I'd like that," said Roy. "But I'd like one here first as well, if I may."

Harold turned to me. "What about you?"

He was mistaken if he thought Roy would bow to an adverse casting vote, as also if he expected me to declare against my principal in the smallest particular. "I must say I'd rather like one, too."

"You mean here as well as at the table?"

"Yes, if that's all right."

After another, slower nod, Harold walked briskly away and out of one of the corners of the room.

"Well played, Duggers. First round to us."

"Do you think it's a good idea to annoy him unnecessarily?"

"Yes. And anyway this is necessarily."

We got our drinks, but it was a technical triumph only. Harold came back as they were handed to us, declined one himself, paid, and stood in silence rather more than a yard off. Although Roy defended stoutly by gossiping to me about musicians and others Harold would not have known even by name, the three of us were in the dining room after a bare ten minutes. A good half of it was occupied by a central table covered from edge to edge with dishes of cold food that not only were clearly un-touched but seemed also inviolable, as at some metropolitan form of harvest festival. We skirted all this and sat down in a corner under a full-length portrait of a duke or other nobleman who, whether or not he had been a fascist, certainly looked the nonpareil of a bastard in general. Menus were before us, and an order pad, complete with carbon paper and uncapped ballpoint pen, lay ready at Harold's side. He led off without hesitation, wrote minutely on the pad and muttered (for publication, so to speak, rather than to himself),

"Tomato salad. Steak and kidney pie. Marrow and French beans."

I noticed that all these items appeared on the clipped-in sheet on which the set lunch, a remarkably cheap package as it appeared to me, was laid out. I said I would have the same, and Harold wrote accordingly. Roy was finding it more difficult to come to a decision, frowning and cocking his head in a style he might have learnt from his wife. Finally he said,

"Tomato salad . . . yes. Then . . . I think duckling and orange sauce. And a green salad."

"Three tomato salads," Harold made an emendation on the pad. "Duckling and . . . Where do you see that?"

"Over here," said Roy with some force, hitting his finger at the *à la carte* section of the menu.

"Oh. Oh, over there. Duckling," said Harold, in the tone, abruptly assumed, of a fanatical vegetarian. He made no move to write.

Roy swept his hand across his front as if cutting off a final chord. "Could I change my mind?"

"By all means."

"I'd like a whole lobster, please, cold, and stuffed with, uh, a portion of caviare. And a green salad, as I said."

"All I'm thinking of is the time. It wouldn't be lined up like uh, for instance, the steak and kidney pie."

"They'll be lined up separately, the lobster and the caviare, and there's no need for the chaps in the kitchen to do the actual stuffing. Get the doings brought to me and I'll stuff it myself."

Harold gave up at that point.

PS: Later, Soref tried very strenuously to make me feel obliged to write his wretched article, so strenuously that otherwise I should probably have kept quiet about the matter except in its disguised form in the novel. Needless to say, no word of any such article ever appeared.

PENELOPE LIVELY

PENELOPE LIVELY

Penelope Lively was born in 1933 in Cairo, where she spent her early childhood. After school in Sussex, she read Modern History at St Anne's College, Oxford. Her work includes eight novels, a collection of short stories and many children's books for which she won both the Carnegie Medal and the Whitbread Award. Two earlier novels were shortlisted for the Booker Prize – *Road to Lichfield* in 1977 and *According to Mark* in 1984 and she won the Prize in 1987 with *Moon Tiger*. Penelope Lively is married to Jack Lively, Professor of Politics at Warwick University, and lives partly in North Oxfordshire and partly in London.

The Children of Grupp

When Trevor Cartwright first saw the Medusa fountain it was the nymphs which caught his attention. Naturally enough. He set down the wheelbarrow for a moment and had a good look; very nice too, all those luscious marble girls. It was his second day as trainee gardener at Rockwell Manor under the Youth Opportunities Programme. He was seventeen; he'd rather have been elsewhere; he wanted farm work, proper stuff with machinery, not messing about manicuring hedges and sweeping up leaves.

The gardens of Rockwell Manor are renowned for topiary and statues. The Medusa fountain, at the end of the famous Yew Walk, is of course the *pièce de résistance*. The Medusa, framed by ferns and the dripping grotto, presides over the great basin of the fountain, at the base of which a charming group of cherubs is arranged in frozen play. Around the rim of the basin sit or recline youthful naked figures – exquisite Apollos and the languid nymphs which appealed to Trevor. The Medusa herself is so encrusted with moss and lichen that she is barely recognisable as a face, while the snakes of her hair have long since fused with the background of rock and greenery. Trevor did not even see her, on that first occasion; in any case he did not like to hang around too long or he'd have Fletcher down on him like a ton of bricks. Fletcher was the head gardener, and a right so-and-so. That he was in fact a first cousin once removed of Trevor's did not qualify his brusque treatment of the newest YOP. So, having taken in the girls and the blokes and all those stone babies larking around in the cool green water – no bad place to be, on a sweltering August afternoon – Trevor upended the wheelbarrow once more and set off towards his next task.

He knew the gardens well, of course. He'd been born and grown up a mile away. The hamlet of Grupp, a dour little collection of tied cottages, has traditionally supplied the labour force for the Manor and its gardens, open to the public since the nineteen thirties. Trevor's grandfather had worked there, and his great grandfather before that. His own father had managed to break out, and got himself into the building trade when times were better. Now, the economic climate had forced Trevor back into the mould; resentfully, he had presented himself at the estate office. His mother, of a more subservient and less querulous generation, had told him off for being truculent: "There's always been a to and fro between Grupp and the Manor. They're funny people, the Saxbys, but they done all right by the village. Back in grandad's day there was estate parties once a year – swimming in the fountain, for the children, and a skittle alley in the stable yard." Trevor was unimpressed.

The present owner, Colonel Saxby, was a recluse, inflated by local rumour to a vaguely sinister figure, for no reliable reason. The wider world certainly found him unaccommodating; art historians interested in the statuary were turned away with a handout to the effect that no records existed concerning the provenance of the various pieces and that photography was not allowed. The figures were of indeterminate age – most appeared to be vaguely eighteenth century, though some of the draped classical ladies presiding over the Yew Walk might well have been earlier. The Medusa Fountain was a puzzle – those experts who had been able to inspect it closely felt that as a group it was not consistent: figures seemed to have been added at different times. Even the cherubs – the adorable children tumbling and laughing around the foot of the fountain itself – appeared to the practised eye to be slightly at odds with one another, some so worn by time that features and dimples had almost vanished, others with their smiles and marble curls still sharply sculptured.

The gardens did not, in fact, attract large numbers of visitors. Advertising was desultory; opening times were capricious. Of those who did come, most were struck by the melancholy atmosphere of the place, an atmosphere that seemed indeed to spill out into the surrounding countryside, so that the dark hedgerows and lowering copses became an extension of the brooding woodland and sombre rides of the Manor gardens. Those who knew no better said that a few good herbaceous borders would have cheered the place up; others, more practised in earlier traditions of gardening, commented on its picturesque qualities but still felt a chill as they plodded down endless vistas between dank hedges from which stared the blank stone eyes of Dianas and Cupids and Apollos. If, on leaving the car park, they failed to take the turn that led back to the main road and fetched up by mistake in Grupp, the sense of gloom and abandonment would be reinforced. The cottages had a sullen look; there was neither shop nor pub. Appearance, indeed, was reinforced by reputation; Grupp people were said to keep themselves to themselves, there was gossip about inbreeding and absence of initiative. Certainly, the hamlet had today a semi-abandoned air; several of the cottages were in derelict condition. Aspiring purchasers from Birmingham or London were turned away at the estate office with a blunt refusal: estate cottages were never put on the market. A demographic historian, attracted by interestingly high infant mortality rates, was met with cold stares and slammed front doors.

Trevor, a child of Grupp, knew only that he yearned for a proper man's job with machinery – tractors and muck-spreaders and combines – instead of which here he was stuck in the gardens with a wheelbarrow and a rake and Fletcher bawling him out if he deviated from instructions for an instant. He found himself working in isolation for the most part, hand-weeding on his knees in remoter regions of the gardens, monotonously raking lawns, trundling barrowloads of debris to the compost heaps. It was a summer of relentless heat and humidity. Employees at Rockwell were required to dress decorously. On his first day Trevor had stripped to the waist, and was roundly abused by Fletcher; thereafter he sweated in his shirt and cast envious glances at the marble nudity all round him – the gleaming torsos, the pale curves of buttocks and breasts, the slender bared limbs. It was all a bit sexy, too, no question about it, could get you quite worked up when you were on your own with them – waving their arses at you from among the trees.

After his first brief glimpse of the Medusa fountain Trevor found himself irresistibly drawn to the spot. He made several illicit detours that day, for the pleasure of a quick splash of the face and hands in the water. There was something gloomy about the place, that was undeniable, but the watery cool of it, and the silver splash of the fountain, compensated for the gloom, while he came to feel the figures positively companionable. One particular nymph became a favourite. There she sat, curled on the rim of the basin with her hand held shyly over her breasts, as though she had been caught out in a private skinny-dip. On first acquaintance he had found her arousing; now, after several visits, he looked at her differently, seeing her beautiful immobility as in some way sad and vulnerable. She seemed to have an expression of eternal shock and surprise in her blank stone eyes; there was a quality in her face that was familiar, too. To be honest, she had a look of his Auntie Marian. Even, ever so slightly, of his own mum.

He became bolder in his visits to the fountain. He lingered for longer, trailed his hands and arms in the water, sat on the rim of the basin for a minute or two, idly splashing. He was tempting providence, and providence inevitably, struck. He had dunked his face in the water and was vigorously sousing his hair when a voice made him spring guiltily upright. "Take a dip then, boy. Go on. Get stripped off. No need to be ashamed of your body – you'd stand comparison with that lot, by the look of you!"

It was the Colonel. Couldn't be anyone else. There he stood, just below the Medusa head – short, stocky, tweed-suited, grinning from the ferns and rocks of the grotto. Creepy, sprung from nowhere like that.

"We're not allowed to," stammered Trevor. "We're not allowed to take us shirts off, even."

"It'll be between you and me," said the Colonel. "Who's to know? Old Fletcher's busy in the greenhouses. You can take your time. Go on, boy – don't be a fool." He bared his teeth at Trevor in what was apparently meant as a smile, and was gone. No wonder people said he was a peculiar old bastard.

Trevor looked around. It was quite true – Fletcher was occupied elsewhere. It was not a public opening day. He was quite alone. He hesitated, then ripped off his shirt, jeans and underpants and stepped into the fountain.

It was wonderful. Deliciously cool, and deeper than you would have thought. He was up to his waist. He waded around, revelling in it. He swam a few strokes. Then he rolled on his back and floated, blissfully, gazing up at the dappled ceiling of leaves that flickered across a pale blue sky. He could have stayed there for ever.

Wiser to cut short the risk, though. Better get going. Reluctantly, he stood up, stepped to the edge, hauled himself out on to the rim and sat with his legs in the water to savour a last few delightful moments. The stone figures around him mirrored the contours of his own pink young body. He glanced, a touch complacently, at his lean torso, his flat muscular flanks, his long legs; what had the old bloke said about comparisons with that lot?

He looked across the pool at the grotto; the Medusa, snake-haired and mossy, stared straight at him. The light seemed to dim, as though the sun had gone in; the frolicking cherubs dulled from gold to grey. It wasn't so warm, either; he started to withdraw his legs from the water. They felt oddly stiff and leaden; maybe he'd got a bit of a cramp. He sat, trying to flex his toes; he seemed to have no sensation in them at all. He could see them, down there in the greenish water, as though they were someone else's.

He reached out for his shirt, lying on the barrow behind him, to give himself a rub down with it. At least, he tried to reach – but now his arm too was numb, leaden, he could scarcely lift it. He hauled it an inch or two – and it fell back inert in his lap. Panic seized him: "I'm ill!" he thought. "I've had a heart attack, like Grandad – I'll die, sat here like this." He tried to shout, and his jaw would not move. He dragged his hand up to his face, with hideous effort; he touched his mouth, saw his fist lie against it, and felt nothing.

He moved his head, inch by inch, fighting his own rigidity; he tried to look towards the great Yew Walk, to see if anyone might be within sight. He could not see that far, but he was looking now at his neighbour on the rim of the fountain, at the nymph, the girl, his favourite, she who shielded her breasts with one hand in eternal modesty. And her stone eyes met his, it seemed, not in shock or surprise but in terrible grief.

He saw the colour ebb from his own body. He saw the delicate veining of marble appear on his thighs. He saw himself become uniform with the nymphs, with Apollo, with the mermaid and the satyr and with the cherubs – those plump children frozen in play at the foot of the fountain, their marble curls touched with golden lichen. Some while after all feeling had left him, when he knew himself to be no longer a creature of flesh and blood but an object deep within which there lurked some awful consciousness of what had once been – sometime then he heard and saw the Colonel. He saw him come again and stand below the grotto, contemplating his possessions. But Trevor had lost all sense of time by then; it might have been the next day, or the next month or the next year. Time would cease to be for Trevor: the seasons would succeed one another as he remained locked within the prison of his fine young body. The snow would lie in ridges along his arms, heap up on his thighs and fill his lap. The summer sun would bake him. The autumn leaves would pile up around him and float on to the surface of the water. He would hear the voices of visitors, the blank globes of his eyes would register their passage – bright moving blurs of colour beyond the rigid presences of his companions, suspended in time, locked in a dreadful eternity of weather and memory. There they would sit and recline, the handsome youths, the graceful girls. And the cherubs . . . Oh, but the thought of the children of Grupp is beyond bearing.

PETER CAREY

PETER CAREY

Peter Carey was born in 1943 in Bacchus Marsh, Victoria, Australia and educated at Geelong Grammar School. He spent a year at Monash University studying science, then joined an advertising agency whose copy department was staffed exclusively with novelists and short story writers. In 1965 he wrote his first novel. But it was not until 1974 – three unpublished novels later – that his first book of stories, *The Fat Man in History*, appeared in Australia. This was followed by *War Crimes* which won him the New South Wales Premier's Award in 1980. His novel *Bliss* won the same award in 1982 as well as the Miles Franklin and National Book Council Awards. His novel, *Illywhacker* (1985) won three major Australian literary awards and was shortlisted for the 1985 Booker Prize. *Oscar and Lucinda* won the 1988 Booker Prize. Peter Carey is married to the theatre director Alison Summers. They have a son. They live in New York.

I choose this piece as a belated thankyou note to the author of *The Satanic Verses*, not the difficult man I read about in *Time* Magazine and the *Herald Tribune* but another kinder man who gave up what no writer ever wants to give up – a day's writing – in order to drive me down to Devon to find the place where Oscar would live.

It was October 1985. I was in London to not win the Booker Prize for *Illywhacker*. I was in the process of writing *Oscar and Lucinda* and although I had done a great deal of library research I had still not made my first visit to Devon. It was Salman, whom I had just met, who drove me down.

It was a chilly day. I sat in the car making bad drawings of the weather. The "thin swathe of soft gold, like a dagger left carelessly lying on a window sill" is grown from the appalling drawing I did in Salman's car.

We found Oddicombe and various othercombes. We stood at the top of the steep combe which I would make gentle enough to let Oscar run down. We walked the paths down which Oscar would speed towards his apostasy, collected pebbles from the beach which are now somewhere in the water off Longnose Point in Sydney, and drank a bottle of good red wine in a dining room with no windows and therefore no view of anything but our own pasts which we were both, in not dissimilar ways, engaged in writing about.

None of this, in the normal course of events, would be worth remarking on were it not for the fact that *Oscar and Lucinda* and *The Satanic Verses* were both shortlisted for the Booker Prize in the same year. When Salman's rich and original novel did not win, the press was loudly amazed that Rushdie had not had another of his "outbursts". The truth is that on this night, already coping with death threats to himself and his family, under more pressure than most of us will ever have to dream of facing, Salman Rushdie was as generous as it is possible for one writer to be about the work of another.

Extract from *Oscar and Lucinda*

A Prayer

Oscar was afraid of the sea. It smelt of death to him. When he thought about this "death", it was not as a single thing you could label with a single word. It was not a discreet entity. It fractured and flew apart, it swarmed like fish, splintered like glass. Death came at him like a ghost in a dream, transmogrifying, proto-plasmic, embracing, affectionate, was one minute cold and wet like his father's oilskin, so he shrank from it and cried out in his sleep, pushing the tight-bunched flannel sheet into the pit of his stomach, and then sometimes it was warm and soft and wore the unfocused smile of his mother.

In the sea-shells on the beach he saw the wonders which it was his father's life to label, dissect, kill. He also saw corpses, bones, creatures dead. Creatures with no souls. When the sea lifted dark tangles of weed, he thought of jerseys with nothing in their arms. He fetched the buckets from where they had stood since autumn, hanging on the back wall beside the well. He did not like the sea to touch his ankles. He felt the light frizzing froth like steel shackles on his skin. He put his fine hands to the pit of his stomach and stood stock still, his face chalky and carved, like a creature wishing to make itself invisible before the eyes of a predator.

Mrs Williams swooped down on him with pullovers. She made him put four of them on, helping him in her breathless, impatient way, pulling his hair by mistake and getting the sleeve of the first rucked up inside the sleeve of the second, and so on, until he was a sturdy lumpy creature with a big woollen chest.

She did not meet his eye or say anything about the pudding.

"What will happen to her?" Oscar asked.

Mrs Williams was not worrying about Fanny Drabble. She was worrying about herself. She took her hairbrush from her pinny and tried to tidy Oscar's hair. It was as bad as her own. Oscar struggled under the sharp bristles.

"I forbid you," said Oscar, and was surprised that Mrs Williams stopped.

"Then go," said Mrs Williams, handing him the buckets and the coil of rope. "Swim," she said maliciously. She knew he was afraid of the sea. He carried his fear coiled and tangled in him like other boys carry twine and string in their crumb-filled pockets. You would not know he had it. You would think him cheerful, happy, obliging, polite. And he was. He was very religious, yes, but not in a gloomy way. When he talked about God it was with simplicity and joy. He had a face better suited to the master's beliefs than the master himself.

Mrs Williams looked into this face to see the fear. She could not locate it. There was something else, but he would not show her what it was.

This something else was anger.

His right ear was still hot and stinging from the blow. He followed his father out of the front gate (bumping it – he always bumped it) and down the steep and sticky path (counting his steps – he always counted) towards the sea, with his anger held hard against him, like a dagger. He took short steps to make the number of steps right. He carried six metal buckets, three hessian bags, a coil of rope, and the buckets banged against his scratched blue shins. His stockings did not have sufficient calf to hold them up; they were rumpled and mixed with red mud around the shiny brown laced boots. He had already torn the seat of his knickerbockers on a bramble and there was more red mud on his woolly combinations. This was a boy, anyone could see it, whose school books would be smudged and blotted. He slipped and stumbled down the path, counting, in the direction of the sea.

It was not marine biology that led Theophilus down this path to stand chest deep in freezing water. He was a naturalist, of course, and he would collect specimens. But now he was in a passion to bear witness. He dug his nails into the palms of his hands. He pulled himself upright by that imaginary thread he kept in the centre of his skull. He would show all of Hennacombe – his son most particularly – what a true Christian thought of Christmas. His breath was shallow and he bore on his face an expression which a stranger might mistake for a smile.

They were still in the mulch-damp dripping woods between the high downs and the sea, but Oscar could already smell death. It was lying out of sight, neat black velvet mounds of it, a weed named *Melanosperm* washed up beneath the fox-red cliff which gave the hamlet of Hennacombe its name. He could also smell the poisonous salt. He was short sighted and could not see any more of the sea than a soft grey colour, like a sheet of satin thrown across a pit. But he could hear it already and knew how it would be, lying flat and docile like a tiger sleeping. It would be grey and pearly and would let itself be drunk up by the sand in quiet fizzy laps. But the *Melanosperm* was there to give the lie to this, to show that the sea could pluck free a plant the strongest man could not dislodge, could kill the man himself, push white plumes down his gurgling throat, tear off his clothes and leave them scattered and formless, pale pink things like jellyfish along the white-laced edges of the beach.

He counted the steps. It was habit. He was hardly thinking about it. If he could walk to the bottom of the cliff in three hundred and sixty-five steps, it would be, in some way, he was not sure, good.

He could still taste the plum pudding which had been denied him so violently. His ear ached and burned, and the anger did not diminish. The anger was unthinkable, but it was not a thinking thing. It took charge of him and shook him. He was a rabbit in its jaws. He slid down the red crumbling combe (count that as five steps) clanging his buckets together, barking his knuckles on the gravel-rough clay.

His father was breathing in *that* way. He wore thick woollen pullovers and a mottled oilskin the colour of burnt toast. Around this he wound belts and ropes to hold his hammers and chisels, his buckets and bags. His father was dark and sinewy, like something made from tarred rope. His father's hair was black, signed with silver fire.

The son's hair was golden red, wiry, always awry. He stood
on the beach (four hundred steps) like an angel, recently landed,
his hair buffeted by turbulent air.

"Fill up," said Theophilus. He should not have hit the boy,
but how else could he prevent the stuff being swallowed?

Oscar began to "fill up". This involved him standing on the
edge of the rust-red rock pool, lowering a bucket, letting it fill,
drawing it up, and then pouring water into the buckets his father
lashed to himself. As the buckets filled his father would groan
with the weight. His groans were comic.

But today Oscar would not look at his father. He was frightened of what those eyes would reveal. He watched his father's
mouth instead. He watched it as if it were a sea creature, a
red-lipped anemone with black hairy fronds. He stood above the
sea as above a pit of hissing snakes.

Then the father walked into the sea. The sea was an amoeba,
a protoplasm. It opened its salt-sticky arms and closed around
the man. It flowed on to the sand and hissed beneath the boy's
boots. He stepped back from it, back above the funereal fronds
of *Melanosperm*, back until the cliff was firm behind his bony
shoulder blades. The clouds were a soft and pearlescent grey,
moulded like sand from which the tide has slowly run out. They
were like a lid, sitting tight on the horizon, except to the south
where there was a thin swathe of soft gold, like a dagger left
carelessly lying on a window-sill.

His father was indistinct, an unfocused dark shape, a lump in
a dream.

Oscar sat like a stook of sticks, a lean-to of too-long bones.
When he hugged himself against his knees, they clicked. He sat
with his back pressed hard against the red cliff, his scrotum tight
with cold, a leathery wrinkled purse with only twopence in it,
the skin tough and thick, like the gizzards of chickens, like the
worm-eaten rock where his father stood, with cold water up
above his chest, chiselling lumps of rock and dropping them into
a wire basket.

Oscar pushed his back hard against Hennacombe Cliff and
while the wind brought a small storm of sand to dance around
his ankles, he talked to God. He did not do this in the distant

and ritualistic way the Anglican Stratton was said to do, with crossing and kneeling. He sat upright. He brought his hands together (one sandy, one smooth) and rubbed them hard as he spoke, unconsciously mimicking his father who, when praying, could be seen to wrestle physically with himself while he tried to hear, amidst all the clamouring costers' voices of his sinner's heart, the pure and uncorrupted word of God.

"Dear God," he said loudly, in a high and fluting voice, "if it is your desire that your flock eat pudding in celebration of Thy birth as man, then show Thy humble supplicant a sign."

He screwed up his eyes and opened them fast. What did he expect? Angels? His friend Tommy Croucher claimed to have seen an angel. He said it was ten feet tall and his mother had seen its head above the milking shed. He took Oscar and showed him what the angel had left behind. There were three small stones which made the points of a triangle. Tommy said they stood for "Father", "Son", and "Holy Ghost". Oscar had not believed Tommy Croucher, but when he saw that the sign was the mathematical symbol for "therefore it follows", he changed his mind.

But on the beach on Christmas Day there was no sign, just the slightest brightening of the golden dagger to the south.

He grunted and rubbed his hands together. His ear was still aching from the blow. The taste in his mouth was vomit, but what he remembered was plums, raisins, cherries, suet, custard made from yellow-yolked eggs and creamy milk. This was not the fruit of Satan. It was not the flesh of which idols eat.

"Dear God," he said, and the straight edge of his teeth showed, "if it be Thy will that Thy people eat pudding, smite him!"

He twisted his limbs around the sandy corridors of prayer. He looked up to see his father almost out of the sea. He struggled to his feet. His knees went click; first the left and then the right, and then he ran, the guilty and obedient son, to help with the little creatures his father had captured, the anemones, antheas with fragile white tentacles, red-bannered dulses, perhaps a sleek green prawn or a fragile living blossom, a proof of the existence of God, a miracle in ivory, rosy red, orange or amethyst.

He ran with his arms flailing, his lower legs kicking out awkwardly. He was not an athlete, but he was at the water's hissing edge when his father emerged, like a matted red-lipped Neptune, blue-nosed, encased in dripping wet wool and shining burnt toast. It was then, as he took the heavy buckets, as he knelt to untie the ropes, that he saw his father had been smitten.

Theophilus's teeth were chattering, his limbs shivering. Red blood came from the wound in his thigh and the instrument, the naturalist's own rock chisel, was still in his hand. Sea water had kept the blood washed away, but now it rose through the blue serge, a thick flower of it, unnaturally bright.

Oscar was no longer angry. He lowered his bucket, frightened of what he had begun.

BOOKER PRIZE
Winners and Shortlisted Authors

1969
P. H. NEWBY *Something to Answer For* Faber and Faber
BARRY ENGLAND *Figures in a Landscape* Cape
NICHOLAS MOSLEY *The Impossible Object* Hodder and Stoughton
IRIS MURDOCH *The Nice and the Good* Chatto and Windus
MURIEL SPARK *The Public Image* Macmillan
G. M. WILLIAMS *From Scenes Like These* Secker and Warburg

1970
BERNICE RUBENS *The Elected Member* Eyre and Spottiswoode
A. L. BARKER *John Brown's Body* Hogarth Press
ELIZABETH BOWEN *Eva Trout* Cape
IRIS MURDOCH *Bruno's Dream* Chatto and Windus
WILLIAM TREVOR *Mrs Eckdorf in O'Neill's Hotel* Bodley Head
T. WHEELER *The Conjunction* Angus and Robertson

1971
V. S. NAIPAUL *In a Free State* Deutsch
THOMAS KILROY *The Big Chapel* Faber and Faber
DORIS LESSING *Briefing for a Descent into Hell* Cape
MORDECAI RICHLER *St Urbain's Horseman* Weidenfeld and Nicolson
DEREK ROBINSON *Goshawk Squadron* Heinemann
ELIZABETH TAYLOR *Mrs Palfrey at the Claremont* Chatto and Windus

1972
JOHN BERGER *G* Weidenfeld and Nicolson
SUSAN HILL *Bird of Night* Hamish Hamilton
THOMAS KENEALLY *The Chant of Jimmie Blacksmith* Angus and Robertson
DAVID STOREY *Pasmore* Longman

1973
J. G. FARRELL *The Siege of Krishnapur* Weidenfeld and Nicolson
BERYL BAINBRIDGE *The Dressmaker* Duckworth

ELIZABETH MAVOR *The Green Equinox* Michael Joseph
IRIS MURDOCH *The Black Prince* Chatto and Windus

1974
NADINE GORDIMER *The Conservationist* Cape
STANLEY MIDDLETON *Holiday* Hutchinson
KINGSLEY AMIS *Ending Up* Cape
BERYL BAINBRIDGE *The Bottle Factory Outing* Duckworth
C. P. SNOW *In Their Wisdom* Macmillan

1975
RUTH PRAWER JHABVALA *Heat and Dust* John Murray
THOMAS KENEALLY *Gossip from the Forest* Collins

1976
DAVID STOREY *Saville* Cape
ANDRE BRINK *An Instant in the Wind* W. H. Allen
R. C. HUTCHINSON *Rising* Michael Joseph
BRIAN MOORE *The Doctor's Wife* Cape
JULIAN RATHBONE *King Fisher Lives* Michael Joseph
WILLIAM TREVOR *The Children of Dynmouth* Bodley Head

1977
PAUL SCOTT *Staying On* Heinemann
PAUL BAILEY *Peter Smart's Confessions* Cape
CAROLINE BLACKWOOD *Great Granny Webster* Duckworth
JENNIFER JOHNSTON *Shadows on Our Skin* Hamish Hamilton
PENELOPE LIVELY *The Road to Lichfield* Heinemann
BARBARA PYM *Quartet in Autumn* Macmillan

1978
IRIS MURDOCH *The Sea, The Sea* Chatto and Windus
KINGSLEY AMIS *Jake's Thing* Hutchinson
ANDRE BRINK *Rumours of Rain* W. H. Allen
PENELOPE FITZGERALD *The Bookshop* Duckworth
JANE GARDAM *God on the Rocks* Hamish Hamilton
BERNICE RUBENS *A Five-Year Sentence* W. H. Allen

1979
PENELOPE FITZGERALD *Offshore* Collins
THOMAS KENEALLY *Confederates* Collins
V. S. NAIPAUL *A Bend in the River* Deutsch
JULIAN RATHBONE *Joseph* Michael Joseph
FAY WELDON *Praxis* Hodder and Stoughton

1980

WILLIAM GOLDING *Rites of Passage* Faber and Faber
ANTHONY BURGESS *Earthly Powers* Hutchinson
ANITA DESAI *Clear Light of Day* Heinemann
ALICE MUNRO *The Beggar Maid* Allen Lane
JULIA O'FAOLAIN *No Country for Young Men* Allen Lane
BARRY UNSWORTH *Pascali's Island* Michael Joseph
J. L. CARR *A Month in the Country* Harvester

1981

SALMAN RUSHDIE *Midnight's Children* Cape
MOLLY KEANE *Good Behaviour* Deutsch
DORIS LESSING *The Sirian Experiments* Cape
IAN McEWAN *The Comfort of Strangers* Cape
ANNE SCHLEE *Rhine Journey* Macmillan
MURIEL SPARK *Loitering with Intent* Bodley Head
D. M. THOMAS *The White Hotel* Gollancz

1982

THOMAS KENEALLY *Schindler's Ark* Hodder and Stoughton
JOHN ARDEN *Silence Among the Weapons* Methuen
WILLIAM BOYD *An Ice-Cream War* Hamish Hamilton
LAWRENCE DURRELL *Constance or Solitary Practices* Faber and Faber
ALICE THOMAS ELLIS *The 27th Kingdom* Duckworth
TIMOTHY MO *Sour Sweet* Deutsch

1983

J. M. COETZEE *Life & Times of Michael K* Secker and Warburg
MALCOLM BRADBURY *Rates of Exchange* Secker and Warburg
JOHN FULLER *Flying to Nowhere* Salamander Press
ANITA MASON *The Illusionist* Hamish Hamilton
SALMAN RUSHDIE *Shame* Cape
GRAHAM SWIFT *Waterland* Heinemann

1984

ANITA BROOKNER *Hotel du Lac* Cape
J. G. BALLARD *Empire of the Sun* Gollancz
JULIAN BARNES *Flaubert's Parrot* Cape
ANITA DESAI *In Custody* Heinemann
PENELOPE LIVELY *According to Mark* Heinemann
DAVID LODGE *Small World* Secker and Warburg

1985

KERI HULME *The Bone People* Hodder and Stoughton
PETER CAREY *Illywhacker* Faber and Faber

J. L. CARR *The Battle of Pollocks Crossing* Viking
DORIS LESSING *The Good Terrorist* Cape
JAN MORRIS *Last Letters from Hav* Viking
IRIS MURDOCH *The Good Apprentice* Chatto and Windus

1986
KINGSLEY AMIS *The Old Devils* Hutchinson
MARGARET ATWOOD *The Handmaid's Tale* Cape
PAUL BAILEY *Gabriel's Lament* Cape
ROBERTSON DAVIES *What's Bred in the Bone* Viking
KAZUO ISHIGURO *An Artist of the Floating World* Faber and Faber
TIMOTHY MO *An Insular Possession* Chatto and Windus

1987
PENELOPE LIVELY *Moon Tiger* Deutsch
CHINUA ACHEBE *Anthills of the Savannah* Heinemann
PETER ACKROYD *Chatterton* Hamish Hamilton
NINA BAWDEN *Circles of Deceit* Macmillan
BRIAN MOORE *The Colour of Blood* Cape
IRIS MURDOCH *The Book and the Brotherhood* Chatto and Windus

1988
PETER CAREY *Oscar and Lucinda* Faber and Faber
BRUCE CHATWIN *Utz* Cape
PENELOPE FITZGERALD *The Beginning of Spring* Collins
DAVID LODGE *Nice Work* Secker and Warburg
SALMAN RUSHDIE *The Satanic Verses* Viking
MARINA WARNER *The Lost Father* Chatto and Windus

JUDGES
(Chairmen in bold type)

1969 **W. L. Webb**
Dame Rebecca West
Stephen Spender
Frank Kermode
David Farrer

1970 **David Holloway**
Dame Rebecca West
Lady Antonia Fraser
Ross Higgins
Professor Richard Hoggart

1971 **John Gross**
Saul Bellow
John Fowles
Lady Antonia Fraser
Philip Toynbee

1972 **Cyril Connolly**
Dr George Steiner
Elizabeth Bowen

1973 **Karl Miller**
Edna O'Brien
Mary McCarthy

1974 **Ion Trewin**
A. S. Byatt
Elizabeth Jane Howard

1975 **Angus Wilson**
Peter Ackroyd
Susan Hill
Roy Fuller

1976 Walter Allen
Lady (Mary) Wilson
Francis King

1977 Philip Larkin
Beryl Bainbridge
Brendan Gill
David Hughes
Robin Ray

1978 Sir Alfred Ayer
Derwent May
P. H. Newby
Angela Huth
Clare Boylen

1979 Lord (Asa) Briggs
Benny Green
Michael Ratcliffe
Hilary Spurling
Paul Theroux

1980 Professor David Daiches
Ronald Blythe
Margaret Forster
Claire Tomalin
Brian Wenham

1981 Professor Malcolm Bradbury
Brian Aldiss
Joan Bakewell
Professor Samuel Hynes
Hermione Lee

1982 Professor John Carey
Paul Bailey
Frank Delaney
Janet Morgan
Lorna Sage

1983 Fay Weldon
Angela Carter
Terence Kilmartin
Peter Porter
Libby Purves

1984 Professor Richard Cobb
Anthony Curtis
Polly Devlin
John Fuller
Ted Rowlands

1985 The Rt Hon. Norman St John-Stevas
Nina Bawden
J. W. Lambert
Joanna Lumley
Marina Warner

1986 Anthony Thwaite
Edna Healey
Isabel Quigly
Gillian Reynolds
Bernice Rubens

1987 P. D. James
Lady Selina Hastings
Allan Massie
Trevor McDonald
John B. Thompson

1988 The Rt Hon. Michael Foot
Sebastian Faulks
Philip French
Blake Morrison
Rose Tremain

COPYRIGHT DETAILS